Logic Strays

Logic Strays

My Quest to Wrangle Torment

Allison Leich, PhD

Disclaimer

This book is not meant to give mental health advice. Further, this is a non-fiction work, and I have endeavored to present all details of conversations and events to the best of my ability and memory.

This is for every person trapped in torment in a world of blithe positivity quotes who feels unworthy of help.

Table of Contents

FORWARD

Although happiness may not be a simple choice and may evade your grasp, please believe in its existence. Pursue it with all your strength, even if your power has dwindled to a mere speck of might. Decades may have passed during which you have barely held on. Your resolve to maintain that grip despite the torment is valiant, magnificent, and inspirational. Keep hanging on. This book details my struggles with mental illness, specifically what has been called Obsessive Compulsive Disorder and anxiety, along with some depressive episodes. I am a Senior Lecturer at a prestigious university and greatly struggled with the decision about whether to remain anonymous due to the sensitive material presented in this book. My conflict over the choice of anonymity is telling, and I will do anything to fight the stigma of help seeking, to get people to openly communicate their struggles and thereby promote mental peace, the most valuable asset of any individual.

As a researcher, I felt inclined to include evidence from literature regarding some of the illnesses that I battled, but instead decided to write this book as much as possible from the perspective of a non-mental health expert struggling to grapple with the horrors of mental anguish. Chapters 1-8 were written prior to my participation in therapy. In writing Chapter 9, I had begun seeing a clinical psychologist weekly. As you will see, my plans to demonstrate my increasing level of functioning became derailed by life tragedies, but nonetheless, I present these different parts of the book as an intriguing comparison between my thought processes before and after therapy and amidst situational and mental crises. I purposely refrained from adding anything significant to the first part of the book after having gone to therapy, so that you may observe my transformation. Conveying that there is a method of escape from agony is my hope for this text. I used to honestly believe I was beyond hope, but I was gloriously mistaken.

As a caveat, this book is not meant to give mental health advice, as I am unqualified to do so; however, I believe that in sharing my experience and encouraging others to do the same, we can conquer this beast. I will unabashedly proclaim the outstanding benefits of therapy. You are worthy of help.

PART 1

In this section of the book, my encounter with the horrors of mental illness is disclosed, along with my musings about this condition prior to receiving treatment.

Chapter 1

$$\begin{vmatrix} 1 & 0 & 0 \\ 0 & 1 & 0 \\ 0 & 0 & 1 \end{vmatrix}$$

WHAT IS IN A SMILE?

I fashioned a promise to myself long ago, that if I survived, I would uncover a way to help other people grappling with this beast. This divulging of my story is my attempt to make good on that promise.

"You will be missed on this team for your optimism."

"You just always had a smile on your face."

"I sooooo wish that I could be as happy as you are!"

On my college gymnastics team, it was customary for teammates to craft warm departing blurbs in sentimental scrapbooks for the graduating seniors. Mine all had the same theme: my happiness.

No one knew. No one could see the suffering, except for me, of course. Beyond these words, will you be able to feel my pain, or will you perceive my struggles as exaggerated? Will you grasp the confusion hiding between my bombastic lines? Would you have been able to tell I was struggling, even if you couldn't possibly know exactly with what and to which degree? If I met you today, would I discern that you are struggling? I hope so. I truly hope so.

$$\oint$$

Happiness is not a choice; I would love to believe that it is, as would apparently many people, considering that this is a common catchphrase. Perhaps the *pursuit* of happiness is a choice, and by pursuit, I mean the decisive resolution to eschew dissatisfaction and run barefoot through the forest, branches lashing your face, half-starved and freezing, while being pursued by a bear and feverishly fighting to persevere in your brawl for survival. Meanwhile, the sun is setting and as darkness looms, hopelessness gnaws, yet you fight because you hold on to the shard of hope within your soul that summons and whispers that the pierced feet, throbbing joints, starvation, domineering fatigue, blustering cold, and sheer terror are still not sufficient reasons to halt and succumb.

Perhaps then the fight for happiness is indeed a choice, but generally when this phrase is espoused, it evokes an image of a person awakening on a Monday morning who encounters a brief feeling of disappointment that the weekend has ceased, along with frustration about returning to a lackluster job. The coffee doesn't taste quite right, and someone honked at them on the way to work, but because of their unfathomably strong self-will, they will "choose to seize the day and be happy." It seems to work for them. Positive thoughts breed more positive thoughts, and by lunchtime, while munching on a homemade lemon bar from the break room, they post "Happiness is a Choice" on Facebook.

This is devastating.

If we construct a mental torment scale from 0 – 10, with 10 being the most intense mental agony any person has ever experienced, perhaps if you are at a 1 or a 2, then it is possible to forcefully ruminate on positive things without professional help and choose not to dwell on that which is depressing. However, for everyone experiencing a 6, 7, 8, 9, or 10, choosing happiness would be akin to asking a person to swim across the ocean, which shouldn't be too difficult since they are "such a great swimmer." Just because a person can plaster on a smile and count blessings, or likewise, just because someone can jump in a pool and swim dozens of laps, this doesn't mean that they can swim the ocean, or suddenly become a "happy person."

My level of such torment through the years is displayed in the following figure.

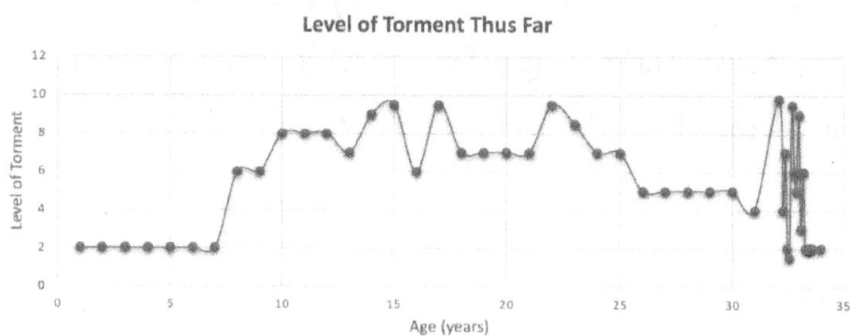

My Torment Scale Index:

0. No troubles exist; the world is a mystically perfect place.

1. The world feels absolutely blissful.

2. Cheerfulness and contentment reign for most of every day.

3. Contentment still exists, yet anxiety has crept forth a bit.

4. The blissful sensation has dulled into a melancholy and worried state. Work becomes difficult to maintain.

5. Most of the day is spent worrying about some calamity, and happiness begins to become arduous to fake.

6. Suicidal compulsions begin to knock daily, but feigning happiness is still feasible, at least for brief social encounters. All strength must be mustered to perform any work tasks.

7. The fear of whether the day will be survivable begins to blaze menacingly, and getting through the day must include escaping to the bathroom to cry and scream quietly.

8. Maniacal swords overwhelm the brain, slashing away at sanity, such that working is impossible.

9. All that is possible to do is lie on the ground and scream in agony.

10. Same as 9 but needing restraining to not repeatedly bash your head against the floor...

I have never discerned a logical reason that I should have experienced any mental torment growing up. I have a loving family. No one even spoke harshly to me. I was deeply loved. I felt like I was treated royally. So every feeling of panic and fear also came with intense guilt, because why should a person be distressed in a perfect life? My grandparents were living in huts in the woods in former Yugoslavia, nearly starving because their homes had been raided and burned down due to wars; my grandfather was thrust out into servitude by the age of 8, and if I am living in luxury in America, how could I confess that I was anything less than thankful and happy?

Chapter 2

$$\begin{vmatrix} 1 & 0 & 0 \\ 0 & 1 & 0 \\ 0 & 0 & 1 \end{vmatrix}$$

THE FIRST WAVE

Perched upon a hotel windowsill and gazing out across the Orlando skyline, I suddenly grabbed my jaw to ensure my teeth were still there. A wafting trace of sulfur escorted an unfamiliar plague through the window, slashing my stomach, and veiling my mind in doom, descending like a dismal vapor upon my 8-year-old form. For whatever reason, I became paranoid that my teeth were going to fall out ... just spontaneously loosen and jettison themselves out of socket. Amidst this fixation, some sort of tormenting internal claw clenched my brain beneath my forehead, boasting of the collapse of the tactile properties of the physical world. Torment is like when you wake up from a ghoulish nightmare, but instead of being able to reason that it was just a dream, the shapeshifting figures and taunting luminosities and monstrosities fail to wane into the morning light. In one day, my feeling of status-quo was rattled by the compulsion to check my permanent teeth every few minutes to make sure that they were not close to falling out. Looking back on it, it seems like such a bizarre fixation, but at least a year vanished into ceaseless apprehension about my teeth.

Our family SUV sauntered down a country road en route to go apple picking in western Virginia. My family sat content in their seats, reveling in the bucolic scenery. A vivacious, youthful song droned in the background, my family tapped their feet along with it, and I mournfully yearned to be happy like that man singing, as lucky for him, his teeth probably weren't falling out.

A few months later, my teeth hadn't fallen out, but as dread seeped through my emotions, I reasoned that neatness and order may protect me from completely disintegrating. During the summer months, my mother worked, so I would spend time at a friend's house during the day. Upon entering their home, I noticed some tattered sneakers and sandals out of alignment near their door, and to halt the din of vexation in my mind, I stooped down and straightened the shoes, so they were aligned and perfectly parallel. Minutes later, the waves of my friend's voice traversed a closed door, as she snickered to her sister, "That weirdo adjusted our shoes!" They giggled with what they thought were hushed tones.

Surrounded by other third graders quietly practicing their writing skills, I ornamented my sheets of wide-ruled paper with a carefully constructed line of text, of which my 9-year-old self was duly proud. Abruptly, the ominous clenching of my brain was manifesting again, and I had to meticulously ensure that my 'O's were perfectly shaped, because whoever my tormenter was convinced me that it would provoke some unknown creature to attack me in the evening, if I went home that night having left subpar handwriting in my cubby.

It began to dawn on me that sleeping may carry a sinister vulnerability. I have a precious friend, Melissa, whom I met as a toddler. While traversing her kitchen during a sleepover, I became terrified of sleepwalking in the night and stabbing everyone. This wasn't a random thought in passing; I was sentenced to spend hours trying to concoct any foolproof plan to be 100% sure that I could never harm anyone in my sleep. I was 9 years old. I was supposed to be having a blast. But how could I have fun knowing that I couldn't control my actions while asleep? Upon surviving the sleepover party and returning home, I beseeched my Mom to hide all of the steak knives in our house—too risky to have them around in case of spontaneous possession. Imagine walking through life with the deep feeling that you may be suddenly overtaken and forced against your will to ravage the planet like a marauder. So any knife had to be avoided by at least 6 feet. Every. Second. Of. The. Day. was spent checking my intentions to ensure I was solid in my love for humanity.

$$\oint$$

Descending from some wicked, nebulous place was that cloak of panic yet again. Somehow the teeth fiasco abruptly ended with the crashing in of a new wave of panic about something more threatening: the fear of any deadly disease. If even a tiny prick feeling struck my intestines, the lights in the room would dim, soft horror music would resonate from an invisible and mysterious source, and my whole body would shake in the grip of doom over the notion that a menacing disease had arisen upon me. It is probably somewhat normal for kids to experience concerns about their body, but this is a large part of what I remember from childhood. Regardless of where I was, birthday parties, school, movies, I was discreetly feeling around my body for any signs of disease.

At ten years of age, my reality purported to be shaped by my fears. Riding my little brother's electronic car in circles around my dad's circular driveway, pondering existence, the wave of vile fright had unceremoniously returned, and I knew I had to reach out and perform the ritualistic search for masses. Suddenly they were actually present. I felt tumors the size of golf balls. Stricken, I dismounted the car and sprinted inside and upstairs into my bathroom and threw up. Collapsing on the bed in horror and sorrow, I groped around for peace. But I couldn't tell anyone, because perhaps going to get tests would manifest death. My dad is a physician himself, and I was terrified of his diagnostic prowess.

What should have been summer fun continued into a family trip to a log cabin; it was an amazing place with a vivacious creek, endless woods, a warm fireplace, and alluring ligneous walls. My jovial family went on memorable walks and roasted marshmallows before the dancing blaze. I was safe. I was warm. I was loved. But I feared the flames would somehow transmogrify into life and engulf me. As the sun would begin to set each evening, I would gear up to not sleep, in order to ensure that tumors didn't overtake me.

$$\oint$$

The vibrant characters and engaging plot of the movie <u>Mulan</u> streamed across the screen of the theater later that summer. I sat beside my best friend, Lauren, analyzing my body for signs of failure.

"Do you want to sleep over tonight?" she excitedly enquired.

I did. But I couldn't handle it.

"Maybe not tonight … "

Surprised, she appealed to our recent fascination with *Happy Days* reruns, *"It will be so fun! We will play games and watch 'The Fonz' rule with his finger snap!"*

I couldn't let her feel bad. I could hide the pain.

Lauren's friendship and perspicaciousness decades beyond her years truly helped keep me fighting for my freedom. Yet that feeling that accompanies a horror movie, with twisted imagery and haunting lights and sounds, waltzed with me unendingly. I can remember how I was treated during this time and the ways my family made my life wonderful, and I still feel guilty about not being able to fully enjoy any of it.

I am thankful for having a decent capacity to remember facts, because throughout high school, I was scarcely able to study; I had to check for diseases between every sentence of reading. For real. Imagine stopping between each of these sentences to check yourself for a disease or assess your mind's stability. Staring at the 47% penned at the top of my "The Adventures of Huckleberry Finn" exam in AP English, I pondered whether I could have recalled more about Huck if I hadn't been obligated to pause every 5 seconds to examine my mind and body.

Was there some significant raft? *Was my mind disintegrating?* I thought there was a river. *Was I worthy of this planet?* There was certainly an important river ... I think.

Mercifully, the teacher weighed my writing more heavily than my abysmal book retention aptitude, and I undeservingly did well in the course.

Throughout my childhood, I never wanted popularity or fame and fortune; I just wanted peace. But peace fled from me.

Sometimes the brain clenching awakened bizarre fears. While walking into my mom's closet, I became convinced that my mom was a fox—the animal ... and of course then I was persuaded that the rest of the planet was a ghoulish version of a real animal, poised to rip off their people masks at any moment and assail me. This type of thought waxed and waned but persistently would bounce back like some kind of freakish magnetic rubber ball in times of stress.

Also raucously present was the fear that everyone was poisoning me. As the trimmings of a thanksgiving feast were delivered to the ornamented table, I awaited the placement of the shimmering water glasses. Wherever I was expected to sit, I would have to watch my glass carefully, lest anyone poison it. (Spoiler: my family would never do such an outlandish thing.) But then perhaps they were this band of covert monster warriors just waiting for the right time? Like your carry-on luggage, which is advised to never leave your sight, my drinks would always need supervision.

Some of my obsessions are perhaps more relatable to those of other people. Like many young girls, I struggled in late middle school with, in addition to the disease phobias, fear of weight gain. Working out vigorously while at home and constantly doing core exercises became my standard behavior. Wistfully sitting in a restaurant and pondering my fitness level, I just knew my life would have more value if I were more toned. I excused myself to the restroom and held myself up on the sinks with my arms in an "L-hold" in order to feel that I deserved to return to my table and consume my food. After enough bathroom calisthenics, I could return to my meal. This became commonplace. I began eating less, forcing myself to stop eating after several bites. Food obsessions and checking for symptoms of fatal diseases congested my mind. Mental mêlées ensued about the food issue. I also became amenorrhoeic for three years in high school in my attempt to control this particular obsession, due to eating scantily. In misery, I combatted the thoughts in the following way:

Thoughts, with a wickedly tranquil tone: "You only think about food; you're a worthless waste of human space."

Me: "I don't only think about food. Think about all the times I had the flu and didn't want food."

Thoughts, methodically, sadistically: "You only think about food unless clouded by a virus; you're a worthless waste of human space."

Me: "But if I cared only about food, I assuredly wouldn't thus worry about it; my worrying about it proves that I am concerned about what I care about, meaning I care at least about caring about something and not being animalistic."

Thoughts: "Granted, you slightly care that you appear normal, but that's just a front so that people will respect you, you will get a good job one day, and thus be able to buy as much food as you want. It's still about your barbaric love of food."

Me: "That's twisted, but I'm not sure exactly how ... "

I never won a debate against my own mind.

Chapter 3

$$\begin{vmatrix} 1 & 0 & 0 \\ 0 & 1 & 0 \\ 0 & 0 & 1 \end{vmatrix}$$

WAS I UNWORTHY OF THIS PLANET?

Lounging nonchalantly on a floral sofa at my dad's house one muggy summer afternoon at the age of 15, the most truculent torment to date ambushed me swiftly and sadistically. No one else was around at the time; the only way I could describe what occurred was that it was akin to being unsuspectingly struck by a dart of peril. This particular fear was of killing myself. I have no idea from where it came, and I was not depressed prior to the onslaught. In fact, I wouldn't have called myself depressed at any point, excruciatingly tormented, but not "sad," "lethargic," or "hopeless." So it snuck up with no warning. Suddenly that sulfuric missile impacted, and I lurched up from the couch and ran to the freezer. So shockingly numb was I, that I desperately tore open an ice cream sandwich and gnawed a Great Dane-sized bite out of it to test whether I could still experience any pleasure. It was as if it turned to dust in my mouth. Panic-stricken, I sprinted up the stairs and paced around for a few minutes before running back downstairs and outside, where I just haplessly wandered, hoping somehow the panic would abate.

It did not abate for 17 years.

Suicide is quite difficult to even write about. Unfortunately, my husband, Jay, first felt suicidal at the age of 7, so in my small world, it seems inescapable. When I had the chicken pox as a child, (the vaccine came out the same summer that I acquired varicella), people always scolded, "Be strong; don't scratch." Even at a very young age, you immediately know what this means. Scratching will be what your brain will tell you to do, but it is in fact wrong; scratching will cause enduring harm to your body, and thus the transient benefit you receive from scratching is pointless. Upon mental distress, the beckoning of suicide feels similar, yet compounded 10,000 times. Self-destruction seems to be the only antidote to the hollow, menacing, vacillating itch.

I cannot point to many things that either helped or hindered my condition, but I do know that intense workouts seemed to be somewhat equally helpful and impairing, ironically. I had read that exercise was stupendous for overall health and stress-free living, but I can definitely attest to the fact that intense cardio workouts were deleterious for my mental state, at least in perception. But I kept believing that sports could be an escape for me; gymnastics provided an adrenaline rush, and perhaps hockey's grueling nature could distract my anguished, muddled mind. I can remember every night during hockey practice, after intense skating drills, crying into my helmet in torment and fear of harming myself once I got home. The increased adrenaline after working out was torturous, but the feeling of movement during exercise was somewhat therapeutic.

I also recall standing outside of my French classroom in ninth grade bawling because I couldn't handle the torment of going home after school by myself and worrying that I might harm myself. But no one knew. The mental severity would range on a daily basis from about a 7 to a 10. On days that it was a 10, I would just clench my head in bed and scream, "Make it stop!" The "it" was the unremitting waves of distress. On days that it was an 8, the food torment would plague me, but ironically, when at a 10, I would absolutely yearn for the food torment in comparison with the self-harm torment. I wondered whether perhaps this was everyone's experience and I was just a weak fighter.

I felt slightly better in tenth grade (maybe at a 7 daily), mostly fearing the food tormenter and having more mental debates against myself about why my self-worth mattered, and whether I cared about something in life more than food. I was slightly less concerned by this point about the tumors, because I reasoned that the fact that they hadn't annihilated me in six years was a good sign.

While crossing through the foyer of my Florida home one day in 11th grade, I just froze, as if suddenly plunged into a glacial sea. The self-harm fear had returned violently, and was seemingly even more nefarious and ominous than I remembered. I tried to attend school. After first period, when I couldn't bear the swords slicing at my face any longer, I told Lauren that my stomach hurt and had to go home. She looked at me quizzically and I wished that I could tell her, that I could ask her to save me. At my school, you couldn't miss more than 8 days of classes and still move on to the next grade, even with excused absences and regardless of having strong grades. Because of this experience, I barely made it through, and ended up with 8 absences that school year. Of course, this was not a concern of mine at the time; my survival was the focus, and the prodigious surprise.

After the freezing episode, it took at least a week before I could go to school. I would tell my Mom that I was too sick to go to school, and it truly was not a lie. I would try. Upon waking, I resolved to fight with all of my might to attend classes, despite the talons of suicidal terror hastening to steal my sanity. I dressed, sauntered boldly out the front door, crossed half of the field between my house and the school, yet furrows of horror overtook my body. I pivoted and dashed ruefully back home for the remainder of the day. It would have been far easier for me to attend school that day with a severe flu and high fever than with that devilish torment. I was a competitive gymnast and was not able to attend practice during this time, due to being "sick" and "weak."

But the world said I could just choose to be happy. So I started worrying that perhaps I wasn't fit to be a member of society. In 6th grade, we had an assignment, most likely a common one, in which we read a story about six people or so in a room with a fatal disease and only one antidote. Predictably, each of the six people had the opportunity to express why they should be permitted to live above the others. There was a young pregnant woman that my classmates chose, since she was effectively two people. There was a famous scientist who was revolutionizing the world, etc. Later, in high school discussing natural selection in Biology and overpopulation in Social Studies, my young, jumbled mind started to seriously ponder whether or not there was some built-in over-population feedback loop somewhere nestled in our genetics that allowed expression of the urge to kill oneself in individuals who were worthless. It was a painfully easy notion for me to believe. As I sat through my classes, with my teachers' voices resounding in the background but never being processed, I pondered this diabolical biology attack theory. I fought the lure to plan to harm myself, and resolved to keep brawling regardless of my pain. Others aren't as blessed to come from loving homes. I was blessed. But still I fought from the moment I awakened each day until the moment I fell asleep against those lustrous tormenting derisions.

Chapter 4

$$\begin{vmatrix} 1 & 0 & 0 \\ 0 & 1 & 0 \\ 0 & 0 & 1 \end{vmatrix}$$

IS ANYONE'S REALITY LUCID?

igh School came and went in a blur, and then childhood was over. For those of you who remember those ever-regressing years of the past, when you play Super Mario Brothers, sometimes you go to these bonus rounds in between levels, where you are awarded a certain amount of time to collect coins, and then you are promptly returned to your game, poised to continue your escapades. At 18, I turned and gazed back at my childhood as if I had been in one of those bonus rooms of the video game, but a ghoulish one of misery and anguish. Curiously, by this point, some days were brighter, maybe at a 5 or 6. On those days, I felt like I had been returned briefly from that chamber of horror, and expected to be 9 years old again, back to everyday life. But 9 years had passed in a flurry, and I had lost all of it to torment. I still felt 9.

Somehow, I did extremely well in high school without the ability to study and would be attending the College of William and Mary in the fall. Unfortunately, a new obsession was brewing. This one felt bizarre to me, like crossing your hands with your fingers overlapping in the wrong configuration while walking in a dark hallway with intermittent blasts of frigid then scalding air. I was somehow concerned about my place in time and space and how I could truly be free given the confines of time. For whatever reason, the concern about what time really meant philosophically caused me to feel as though I was being held underwater and only permitted to breathe one shallow breath every 2 minutes while erratically being forced to dance back and forth between spheres of space without time, and spheres of space with time. But in a wild providential stroke, I met a guy who sort of understood my outrageous thought processes, a remarkable young man, a dashing gymnast named Jay whose connection with me dampened my level of torment to about a 5 or 6 for most of my undergraduate trek.

William and Mary was a fantastic place for the development of critical thought. It was certainly a struggle to do well amidst the mental anguish I constantly fought, but I was coherent enough to attest to its prestige in having a strong physics program. I also did gymnastics in college; I love the sport, but it predominately served as a means of escape from the torment I felt. Sometimes during intense workouts, I could briefly subdue the stabbing thoughts. My coach was a comforting person—palpably honorable, pragmatic, and brave, which I admired. But again, the painful workouts would leave a bitter aftertaste of enhanced torment. In this way, intense exercise is somewhat like an addictive drug with distressing side effects.

$

I swung down between the bars in reverse grip, and on the way back up in this front giant, peeled off of the rail and careened toward the ground, my form outstretched and head analyzing the location of the forthcoming floor. Time slackened, and the world's audio adjourned. Still rotating slightly, I continued to gaze at the ground and then considered my options. I could slam headfirst into the mat and wreck myself, or flip myself over. Thankfully, I chose the latter, and as time and sound sputtered back into place, I smacked the earth in a seated position, one foot slamming onto the other, with a painful and nauseating thud. For those milliseconds, I was not tormented.

$$\oint$$

In the classroom, I majored in Physics, mostly because Calculus dazzled me and whimsical Physics teachers in high school had inspired me. Further, it seemed like it would be the hardest major to try. Given my battles at the time, I genuinely believed a person should choose the hardest, most treacherous path set before them, and in that way become a warrior of the world. I was an excellent public speaker and loved to write as well, but was unsure where that could lead. One of my professors freshman year at WM loathed my writing style, sneering, "I don't want to tell you to drop out of school and work at McDonalds, but your writing has to get a LOT better." Perhaps he will read this book and believe that I should not have written it.

Discussing time dilation in Modern Physics did not help my torment about space and time and the curiousness of biological organisms wafting through it. One time during that class, someone was adjusting the building's clocks, and the hands on the clock in the room (those quintessential oatmeal-colored classroom clocks) began actually revolving rapidly, and the professor comically pointed it out as an example; everyone erupted in laughter. I was amused and troubled. Were they all laughing because normal time made sense to them? Quantum Mechanics perhaps made me feel a little better; maybe the world was just incomprehensible, and so as long as you could just make everything look something like a simple harmonic oscillator, then you could estimate the answer to life's problems.

Rapidly and jarringly, college ended.

Chapter 5

$$\begin{vmatrix} 1 & 0 & 0 \\ 0 & 1 & 0 \\ 0 & 0 & 1 \end{vmatrix}$$

INSANITY

Yearning to just endure, I hadn't thought deeply about what I should do after graduation. I really did not have the mental fortitude to worry about it. Plus, when I became concerned about having to find a way to feed myself, the feelings of panic about only caring about food came rushing back with vitriol. Jobs were scarce at this time (2009). In fact, at our college graduation ceremony, one professor spouted,

"Congratulations. You won't be able to find a job, but at least you will be able to rationalize it."

I did find a job teaching Algebra at a private school. It was such fun to teach, but the academic year swiftly became a hellish furnace. The year was still 2009, the fall of which brought that swine flu which struck many people. I got the flu, no big deal, but unexpectedly, while lying in bed quite ill, was socked by the burliest self-harm compulsion to date. I had perceived the torment at a 10 previously but somehow felt even more vexed at this moment, like my skin was ablaze and suicide would be akin to wading into a frosty brook. From that moment on, I drudged through my days scarcely able to eat (because food dissolved to dust in my mouth once again). I would pinch myself all day long, sometimes giving in to the urge to claw at my legs as a painfully blissful distraction. My soul had notably departed my body, and I was watching myself from above, a forlorn person whose mind I observed deteriorating into insanity.

Perceived madness feels like the sprint after a thief who has stolen your purse holding all of your life's worth, and the bandit keeps changing colors, the lights in the room become as strobe lights, ethereal music resounds, the room spins, and you begin to doubt that it is even worth it to pursue your prized purse. Is it even yours? But pursue I did, because I held onto the elusive grain of hope that one day it would all be worth it.

People expressed that I had the greatest smile. I felt like a hollow painting. I sympathize with all of you who have gone through any torment without a smile; not having resting smile face must be even more demoralizing, as the world loathes a frown. After all, why can't we just choose to be happy?

The world thence insidiously began to appear "off." The walls would ever so slightly dim and festoon themselves with carnival-like pennants. I would gaze down at my fingers, and they would elongate into ghastly, thin and pointy appendages. I somehow began feeling unlike a human being, but instead like a worm. I was surely a worm. It didn't make sense that I filled up such a large amorphous state and felt like I should be in the shape of a worm instead.

Working became impossible in late October of 2009. I was not able to care that I would make no money during that time. Bedridden with intense mental confusion, I seldom had a coherent thought. After a while, I did venture from the house, but only to do intense runs and sprints in attempt to evade this wraithlike misery. I couldn't handle life, and shrieking about my torment to my dad and stepmom, from whom I had so gracefully hidden my torment but could no longer sustain the charade, my stepmom took me to see a psychiatrist at age 22. Lying in bed with my frazzled head turned to stare at the clock, I questioned whether I would make it to the appointment. I gripped my phone in my hand, trying to not call 911, with my body trembling and head feeling like a demented firework display of confusion signals. Dawn came slower than usual, and I just sullenly lay there, trying to corral the swarming thoughts.

Within the pallid psychiatry waiting room, I studied the faces of the patients for signs that they were crazier than me. However, their souls seemed to reside within the realm of their bodies just fine. This room felt dimly lit, and the décor was hazy, as if purposely reminiscent of the universal hues of anguish. When finally called, I rushed out of the waiting room into the office and descended into a chair, expecting to be committed to some mental institution. The psychiatrist asked me to explain what was troubling me, and with darting eyes, I explained that I felt confused about my very existence on the planet and that I felt detached and bewildered about how I could still be inside my body. To my astonishment, he remained calm and was not noticeably surprised by my screed. Finally and seemingly randomly, he asked me if I ever had concerns about not swallowing properly while sleeping, and I sputtered, "Sure." He responded, "Well it looks like you're over-thinking everything" and that it was a good thing that the weird thoughts were still fresh and deeply troubling. Maybe he felt as though if I were expressing the same notions, but without fright, that I would have appeared more delusional? He quickly judged that it appeared I had Obsessive Compulsive Disorder. He prescribed Xanax and Lexapro. I was astounded that he did not think I was going crazy.

The Xanax was shockingly powerful; I had become accustomed to the sensation that nothing on the planet could tweak the way my brain felt, for better or worse. I was still vexed and confused, but the Xanax seemed to enable me to sleep a bit better and perhaps relax marginally, with the added bonus of introducing a sickening sensation of lying on a boat, rocking forcefully in the outer bands of a hurricane. However, this oddity was a kind alternative to the incessant daggers of fear piercing my skull. The torment seemed to improve from a 10 to a 9.3 while I was on this medication. Of course, I was told that it should only be used temporarily, and so I stopped taking it, at the direction of the psychiatrist, abruptly after 2 weeks.

Disconnecting from this drug provides an intriguing experience. Every three or four seconds, I would feel electrocuted, a distinct shock centered on the top of my head and twisting down through my spine and limbs. Because of my desperation to feel anything at this time, it was both terrifying and encouraging. The Lexapro had not noticeably changed anything at this point, but I kept hoping. Meanwhile, the confusion I experienced constantly was akin to waking up from a nightmare as a child, confused about where I was. It would take a few seconds to rekindle the feeling of "me" and re-center myself with an understanding of my surroundings and reality. This return to reality was now elusive to me; I would stare down at my arms, feet, and hands and just be so confused about how I inhabited this body and how it had not troubled me previously. Should I remove my arms and legs? I felt like I did not understand how to talk or write or walk, although I would painstakingly force myself to do these things and be astonished at my apparent success and outward appearance of normalcy.

Chapter 6

$$\begin{vmatrix} 1 & 0 & 0 \\ 0 & 1 & 0 \\ 0 & 0 & 1 \end{vmatrix}$$

PERCEPTIONS

I certainly cannot claim to have a solution or even a suggestion for every soul trapped in torment, but in hopes that my discovery may unearth a token of truth for just one individual, I assume it is worth my while to write this book. What I discovered as I trudged through my days in confusion and perceived insanity was that there was what felt like a time delay of my conscious mind. Two parts of my consciousness felt hacked; the first part damaged felt like that computer program in yourself (which executes automatically) that has been developed from your personal experiences, choices, and genes that comprise the basic decision-making skills and ability to essentially act as a normal human. The second is the distinct feeling of "you." We feel alive, conscious, and important, and when this feeling of "you-ness" wanes, it is a profoundly terrifying experience that is likened to how you expect death to feel. I've read about that rare disorder where people truly believe they have died. This does not seem far-fetched at all to me. I felt vacant.

During the time of my distress, I used to wonder what indeed made me "me." It baffled me that if I found a picture in one of my school yearbooks of some friends, and I was in the background of the picture, the specific segment of my body that was in the picture changed whether you would say that that was me or a just a part of me. For instance, if a picture of three smiling girls appeared, and a sliver of a purple backpack of mine was showing, you would certainly define the picture as three girls and my backpack. If only my feet were in the picture, it would be the three girls and my feet. If my hand were in front of the camera, or even my arm, it would be the three girls and my arm. But if even a portion of my face were in the picture, it would be four girls (one of whom has a partial face in the photo).

When people say, "Look at me!" they generally mean that they hope you will look at them in the face. If you stare at their chest or legs or arms, they do not feel that you are gazing at whatever makes you "you." I believe that we project a feeling of identity into the area of our chest and above through our face, and everything else just feels like our belongings, like we inhabit this body and our perception of reality is centered in a certain region.

This all may seem obvious, but it is the very core of what I felt was stolen from me during this time. Again, I suppose I believe that there is this processing center within us that is comprised of our genetic makeup, our biological involuntary responses, and also our personally chosen goals which have been filed away electronically for future use. So this processing center surely is like a computer. When you purchased it, it already came with certain functions and software. You also chose to add things to this device (photos, documents, bank statements, etc.) that you felt would be important for the future. But consciousness is like the feeling of being human and your feeling of choosing what you are doing. I do believe that we choose and have free will, but I believe that sudden immediate choices stem more from what we saved to our hard drive than what we feel in a moment (like how being a gymnast trained to fall correctly allows for "subconscious" decision-making before a splat).

I used to be very frustrated with the confusion of how I could sit on a couch and rise and leave the room. It sounds absolutely ridiculous, but thoughts like this rendered me incapable of doing anything. If I could force myself up and out of the room, what I would notice is that I would feel quite confused while I was doing it but nonetheless not staggering or visually appearing strange. I had a program to do this simple maneuver subconsciously, but allowing my conscious mind to take part in the manifestation caused confusion.

Conceivably, there was some strange disconnect in communication between my conscious and subconscious, a half-baked weirdness directed at me like an ancient message in a bottle, stained and barely visible, but clearly something so momentous that I must decipher it; so I conscientiously began to, with every thought and about every 3 seconds every day, shut my eyes and do my best to cling frantically to what I "knew" to be the truth. I felt like the crazed, menacing thoughts taunting me consciously were reality, but somehow, I still "knew" they were not real. Reality feels like a still voice in the pit of your belly that is devoid of colors and sounds and fanfare, but is firm and resolute. Choosing to focus on reality sounds obvious and easy, but it is the furthest thing from apparent or simple when going through torment or a carnival "fun house" and every visual cue is distorted. The second part to what eventually helped me was to forcefully "not care" about whatever the thoughts were telling me. I did in fact care, and do not suggest that it is wrong to care about, for instance, avoiding deadly diseases. But I would have to tell myself, in the sense of screaming at my brain to send that signal, that I in fact did not care what happened. The caring about living or dying or going crazy or being broke was presumably already filed away somewhere; maybe it didn't need to be resurrected in the consciousness?

Chapter 7

$$\begin{vmatrix} 1 & 0 & 0 \\ 0 & 1 & 0 \\ 0 & 0 & 1 \end{vmatrix}$$

CAN ANYTHING RIVAL DESPAIR?

Although while in the depths of despair I was barely able to notice that anything provided even trivial improvement, if my memory serves me, a few items strike me as having been marginally beneficial.

Listed below are things that could very possibly have helped just a bit, or would have helped, had I been provided with them ... Like BARELY helped! Nothing really helped very much, but I was fishing for a memory of something that felt like it had just a tinge of promise (for me). This is 100% NOT one of those "keys to mental success" lists. It's a personal reflection that may provide you with interesting patterns on my experience but wouldn't necessarily have the same effect on you.

Those very marginally beneficial things:

1. **For anyone to listen to the existential obsession and point out an error in my logic ...** or if they couldn't, to at least say something about this being a fantasy world of sorts. The best thing would be for someone to acknowledge that there is some philosophical gold in my troubled thoughts but that my logic has been found wanting.

2. **Standing in the shower and suddenly turning the water down to a frigid temperature and then quickly turning the temperature back to very warm.** Perhaps the brief shock of the wintry

weather supplied 0.2 seconds of forgetting the agony.

3. **Xanax.** It's horrifyingly dangerous. It just makes the list because it was indisputably potent enough to provide a slight change.

4. **The feeling of falling ...** like when you jump on a trampoline and are on the way down. The only problem is that maintaining the jumping motion in order to enjoy the brief falling sensation was too tormenting.

5. **Being told "Logic Strays,"** by a friend, Jonathan Sellers

6. **Being questioned.** "Counting blessings" is agonizing, because everything has turned to ash and feels the same: dusty and dismal. But if you interrogate me about scenarios like, "Which is

worse: falling into a cactus or being locked out of your house in freezing weather in flip flops?" ... well, being forced to rank such scenarios somewhat reintroduces tiers to the life experience ... that perhaps everything isn't totally exactly the same drab hue.

7. **Accelerating in a car ... feeling the force of the seat on by back**

Things that definitely hurt!

I. **Any statement sounding like "Just be tough" or "Mind over matter."** Actually, these statements can transform from irksome to motivational if the person spouting them is also willing to support your weight while you work on this "mind over matter" business, even if it takes decades.

2. **Suggestions like "Do Pilates" or "Go for a walk."** If you haven't suffered from mental illness, you may not understand, but deep torment at the level of a 9 or 10 is such that being asked to put on a smile and walk to the mailbox at the end of the driveway, get the mail, and return, would be like asking you to run a marathon with two broken ankles, extreme dehydration and starvation, and while on fire. There is no latte or dance class for that feeling.

3. **Food in general.** Food becomes insipid for me during extreme distress, and leads to a hollow longing for the previous solace that an ice cream cone was able to provide.

4. **Work in general.** Nothing is worse than adding a feeling of entrapment to the sensation of suicidal ideation.

5. **Reading self-help books.** All the ones I read put together templates of how most people with anxiety and depression seem to feel, none of which

I related to. So perhaps I was thus beyond help. People should be told to not ever give up, but probably with the undertone of "This will be the hardest battle you have ever fought." Accordingly, "I will fight this battle alongside of you" ... as long as that person follows through indefinitely. Now that would be helpful.

6. **Exercise?** This one is tough to explain - Exercise is touted as a panacea. During my youth, I went from seasons of working out very little (like only in PE class) to periods of training 20-25 hours per week. I did not perceive much of a difference in morale when increasing or decreasing exercise amount, except for doing weightlifting. Any circuit workouts involving weights were incredibly triggering for me. I have no belief that this would be the experience of everyone, but as someone with extreme anxiety, I could easily detect that the weightlifting exacerbated the torment. Running also had a deleterious effect; I felt like I was being chased by some nebulous and nefarious entity. No amount of mental gymnastics allowed me to stop the "fight or flight" response when doing these forms of

exercises. During terrible times, I would work out obsessively with the goal of quieting the torment, but the exertion would often make me feel more tortured after finishing.

7. **Car trips — especially driving slowly and steadily or blazing down an interstate ...** basically driving at constant velocity is difficult. In any case, I would have crippling urges, with notions of a sickly friendliness of demise pirouetting with dread and lucidity, to open a car door and just roll out onto the road. It is quite difficult to even write that statement.

8. **Any variation of "I have no idea how anything could ever be that bad that someone would hurt himself."** This is such a delusional statement. As someone having experienced extreme torment and lack thereof, it is indeed hard to imagine during periods of peace how your brain could conceive of death as more desirable than anything else. But the fact that it does happen should be proof enough and convincing of the fact that in the throes of the

inky vexation, it is almost unbearable to hold your head above the mire after having treaded for years. This may very well be an illusion, but one that is frighteningly real to its victims. If you have ever found yourself having a brutal nightmare and somehow come to the realization that it is in fact a nightmare and try to coax yourself out of it, it is equally, if not more, petrifying than those ghoulish dreams that have you fully convinced you are in them. Why? Because there is seemingly a way out, but you feel incapable of finding it.

9. **Happy music** — Anything with a happy tone was demoralizing and perturbing. Sad, mournful sounds inched towards helping a bit.

10. **Bright colors** — Modern cartoon movies were particularly depressing; the psychedelic colors taunted and laughed about how beautiful a world it was; clearly, I didn't belong in it.

11. **Being advised to help others/think of others** — If you find yourself starved of oxygen and floundering for breath, no matter how altruistic, you will not be able to help others until you satisfy your urgent need for air. You may be speeding to the hospital to give a life-saving operation, but lack of gas in the car will derail the whole process. If the physician stops for gas to make it to the hospital, no one would say, "The stranded physician should have thought more about her patients than herself," but this is what some do to the mentally ill. After all, a car without gas still sort of works. You can still roll it downhill. The struggling people exist in bodies likened to cars without gas. They look fine: shiny and healthy, but they can only roll downhill. Somehow, we must find gas for them.

Chapter 8

$$\begin{vmatrix} 1 & 0 & 0 \\ 0 & 1 & 0 \\ 0 & 0 & 1 \end{vmatrix}$$

FINAL MUSINGS BEFORE THERAPY

Sadness seems to correspond with cultural perceptions of depression. But sadness is not something that ever caused me grief. Watching a movie that brings me to tears soothes, persuading me to relish the important aspects of life. Sad things that happen in life, like job loss and financial issues, do not wander close to whatever this ghastly and portentous "thing" is. Perhaps I have not ever experienced depression and only had anxiety, but whatever it was that I experienced carried raging thoughts of self-harm, and never sadness. Hopelessness is also a common theme, but it is a tricky concept.

Depression, or whatever this mental torment was, felt like being forced to hang onto infinitely long monkey bars suspended over a pit of lava, with people cheering me on not to let go, but letting go didn't seem like much of a choice. Sure, I felt hopeful that someone would save me, but my hands were so sweaty, the heat from the flames laughed menacingly as my body temperature escalated, and my forearms burned. Despite hopefully fighting to hang on, at some point, anyone's grip would fail. Perishing would feel like just that: slipping out of complete exhaustion ... not a physical action of self-harm.

Usually people being evaluated for mental distress are asked whether or not they have ceased to enjoy things that they once loved. This is also a challenging question to answer, because amidst this type of agony, it is impossible to evoke a memory of ever having loved anything. If I could have done the impossible, reminiscing about the feeling of enjoying something while frantically clinging to that abysmal fire pit rail, that would have provided solace, but I was powerless to reject the lie that my previous interests were never really interests at all, and that I was truly a leaden failure of a human with a slipping grip.

Keep fighting.

Fatigue and insomnia are also often considered. During my worst episodes, I never felt physically tired and usually continued to sleep through the night. Sleeping never felt like a respite, however, as waking up presented an immediate continuation of the previous day with no mental resetting. Muscularly, I felt rested, but my brain had not relaxed for even a moment, concocting escape strategies through the night, while the rest of my body recharged.

Surprisingly, it feels more distressing to partake in activities that should require very little effort, such as parties, trips to amusements parks, etc. than to engage in physical labor. Somehow it is comforting to feel like the one with the most endurance. I enjoy crushing my friends at pull-ups, and I feel a twinge of glee when everyone else appears famished and fatigued. But while playing a game? There is pressure to have fun. What kind of person feels torment when having fun?

Mental distress feels sort of like pedaling up an extreme hill. But perhaps not, because this scenario implies that something is physically pushing back on your fatiguing rectus femoris muscles. Pedaling uphill is brutal, yet there is a confirmation that you are doing something fierce: needing to pedal much more rapidly than your body can activate those motor units. You demonstrably combat the resistant forces, and other people can grasp your strain. Perhaps torment feels more like pedaling downhill—no physically apparent stress—no measurable pain—but your feet are chained to pedals sentenced to rotate with the wheel, so they spin wildly as others nonchalantly glide through the breeze, and you careen turbulently out of control.

PART 2

Please note whether any perspective change exists after starting
therapy!

קנה־חכמה מה־טוב מחרוץ וקנות בינה נבחר מכסף

"How much better to get wisdom than gold, to get insight rather
than silver."

Chapter 9

$$\begin{vmatrix} 1 & 0 & 0 \\ 0 & 1 & 0 \\ 0 & 0 & 1 \end{vmatrix}$$

THE SHOCK OF THERAPY

Nine years had swiftly passed since college. In determination to be successful despite my tormentor, I had strategically selected a quantitative bioscience PhD program in which I could spend my days in a dark corner crafting computer codes, where no one would hear my sobs. Jay had graciously supported me through my mental crises; we had been married since 2010.

I lingered at the dinner table with my stepmom, lamenting over whatever obsession du jour oppressed me. She gazed at me with concern and leaned back slightly before declaring:

"You really need to talk to someone about this."

I immediately knew what she meant. She thought I needed a therapist. But could a therapist help me? Would they actually want to help me? How long would their patience last? Would I be considered weak for seeking help? Are my problems just of the sort that are common to humans, but some win their own battles and others need an army? What if they couldn't help me? ... that would indisputably solidify my feelings of doom.

Especially since she gave me money to initiate therapy, I struggled to find a solid reason to ignore her counsel to do so. After all, I could just go for a few months to appease her and then gracefully bow out, right?

It started with a Google search for "psychologist in Nashville." Among the top website suggestions was this "Psychology Today" site where practitioners post blurbs about themselves and list the seemingly recondite therapeutic strategies that they employ. I clicked the *Aetna* insurance box, along with *Obsessive Compulsive,* and was greeted by the smiling faces of willing practitioners. Like scanning a clothing rack from afar in a department store, I waited for something to jump out at me. The one who made that jump was called Joe. Nestled in his profile text was the phrase that he didn't believe that he "worked on people" but "with people." I sorely wish I could recall what else the page said, but his ambiance felt right. I made the call.

The first session was momentously intimidating. I brought Jay with me for support and tried to suppress the sneering terror dragging me in the other direction. Sneaking up and yanking my reality once again, that woefully familiar detachment from my body caused me to seemingly flit down the hall toward that fateful office. We located Joe's office and sank into some couches across from the closed door. This door was intimidating, long and narrow, stretching from floor to ceiling in an antediluvian brown hue. Panicked does not even begin to describe the state of my brain at the time. I anticipated being greeted by this omniscient being who would undoubtedly immediately scan my mind and propose that I be committed to some hospital for my aberrant thoughts. Eventually that pivotal door creaked, opened, and out emerged a relatively young, professionally dressed man with steady and sympathetic eyes. Greeting us warmly without staring me down, he escorted us into his office. Within the room sat his desk, and two kingly armchairs adorned the corners. I was slightly relieved to see that there was a palatial window in the room, as I often feel claustrophobic.

Joe sat down, faced me, and with an unmistakable poise and vigilance, enquired, "What has been going on?" I began to speak, but as usual, felt confused about how the words were rolling out of my mouth.

I continued talking (all the while wondering whether or not I was being coherent) about the intense fears and obsessions with which I have struggled for my entire life. At the end of about 20 minutes of speaking frantically, while it felt like wildebeest were stampeding across my abdomen, I shrunk back while asking him what he thought was wrong with me. Pausing to construct his words, Joe stated, "Well, it's in the OCD family. I can't give you a prediction about how many sessions it will take to see a noticeable reduction in anxiety levels ... Like I can't say if it will be 10 sessions for instance before you feel a 50% reduction in anxiety."

"Ok Great!" I thought. "Perhaps I can be cured in 10 sessions ... "

Thus I went back. Weekly. An interesting pattern emerged. At the initiation of every meeting, Joe would say, "How has everything been going?" I would respond with the same predictable description of how the week had gone. I usually had an appointment on a Friday. (I called myself the Friday lunatic, which seemed to amuse him.) When entertained, he would chortle and then proceed to laugh deeply while still looking forward at me, then turn his head to the right with a slight head tilt and continue the deep laughter.

I often would express to him that the weekend would be tumultuous; I would endure more panic than normal, which would abate on Monday, after which brief feelings of a calmness that I hadn't experienced before would introduce themselves. Therapy sessions seemed to whack at my amygdala and breed fear like a strenuous workout wrecks the muscles but leads to strengthening in the proceeding days.

So in my view, how does therapy feel?

It feels like peeing in the ocean. It's not an analogy that makes much sense besides the feeling of it. Have you ever played in the ocean? At some point you had to pee, but were having too much fun being swept off your feet by pummeling waves, spitting out sea water, and scraping your feet on perplexing ocean floor entities and equally abhorred the notion of using one of those dank, taunting Porta-Potties lining the beaches that hurled their unpleasant odors at unsuspecting passersby within a remarkable 25 foot radius. It is then that you either come to the conclusion yourself or your parent lets you in on that delightful secret. You can pee right here. Right now. No one will know. It won't hurt anything. Alas ... you cautiously start. You let out a trickle and it feels heavenly. So you let out a little more until you are overcome by the contrast of the warmth of your urine and the chill of the ocean water swirling around your legs. As it floods out, you watch the faces of those near you for any sign of insight into your catharsis, and people generally appear unaware. It is an indelible experience that I imagine that other people remember and love as well.

Therapy somewhat resembles this, because you are free to divulge your deepest pain, your secrets, and unspeakable fears and angst without fear of judgment. Shockingly, nearby beach frolickers continue to play, oblivious to the proximate wave urinator (unless you're too close).

$
$

Meanwhile, Jay was out of work due to recurrent, nebulous health issues and depression. He had battled chronic fatigue for years now, and by this point could not usually get out of bed for longer than an hour or so in a given day. He had developed inexplicable whole-body joint pain and severe depression to the point that I would worry all day long during work whether or not I would find my precious husband alive and well upon returning home. So I began to wonder again if I really needed therapy in comparison to him. However, I reasoned that continuing to heal myself would be of benefit to him.

So therapy carried on. Joe asked that I make a list of the topics that distressed me the most, in order. At the top of the list was random panic about having cardiovascular issues. I had begun to avoid walking up the stairs at work, because any acceleration of my heart could trigger a panic attack. Also on the list was my fear of being without food. I had had some issues with feelings of hypoglycemia in the past, invoking dizziness and confusion, so I became obsessed with making sure there were extensive provisions in my large satchel at all times. Of course, the other food-related issue persisted. In being overwrought about having food all the time, I explained to Joe, I became concerned that all I cared about was food, like an animal whose day centers only around how they can chow down, and that my life thus had no meaning.

I also described my issues with irrational contamination worries. I obsessed about whether my shoe, while out and about, had absorbed some sort of nefarious chemical, and then I tracked the chemical all through my house later that day, dropped a piece of paper where I had traversed, picked up the paper, and poisoned myself ... and other similar variations. I also would have to wash my hands repeatedly while commanding voices shouted at me that I must do it over and over again in order to avoid something malevolent. I did tell myself, "Hey!! I have a PhD in a science; I probably shouldn't be petrified if I can't define by what mechanism these imagined threats could harm me," but to no avail. Regarding this, Joe had concocted a "disgusting scale":

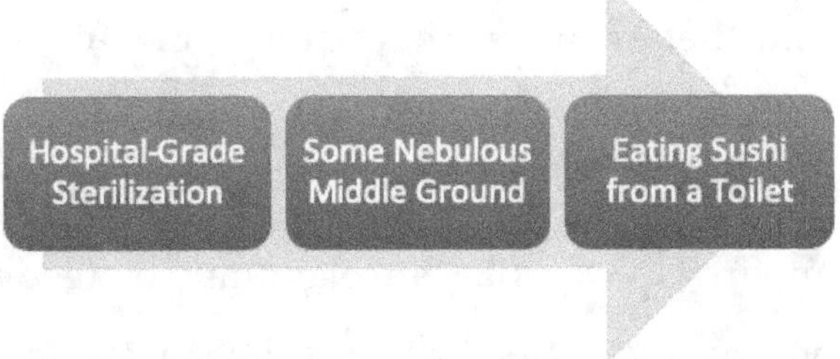

He endeavored to guide me somewhere closer to the middle of this spectrum.

Anyway, Joe suggested beginning with this contamination issue. I heeded Joe's advice to stop the excessive hand washing and just pushed through the pain of ceasing this compulsion. So there were all of these intense itches on my body again, so to speak, and I could not scratch them. As predicted, after the menacing feelings eventually passed, I began to sense a surprising warmth and strength, like the sun rising 4 hours before it is due. Terror began to dim in the light of whatever this new peaceful feeling was. I am unsure whether or not I really understood what even slight peace was prior to this therapy experience.

It was initially helpful to fight the contamination actions. In not engaging in this compulsion, I began to understand better what the pattern of this OCD torment actually feels like in real time, that woeful brain clenching that seemingly lights my prefrontal cortex on fire. It was like an elaborate biofeedback revelation for me, after which I began to adeptly pinpoint other areas in life in which I was thinking irrationally. I also began to take the stairs at work (and there are a ton! It is as if my office were at the top of a lighthouse). The peaceful feeling which worked to unshackle me from the handwashing was also working to slay my panic upon normal exercise-induced heart rate acceleration. I would say that I had at least a 20% reduction in anxiety after about 5 sessions, but would it remain long-term?

Things were looking up, but would the peace last? Now, instead of wondering when therapy could be over so that my wallet wouldn't protest as much, I began to feel somewhat dependent. In between sessions, a new worry hit like a familiar brick wall. Therapy was helping so much; what would I do if I were suddenly dropped from the practice, for being annoying? So naturally, I imagined myself charging into Joe's office and ravaging it, pulling psychology books out of the bookshelf and tearing them to pieces, and afterward hurling Joe's chair through the window to break it while he watched it shatter, sobbing. How disgraceful would that be? What if I went nuts and did this outrageousness? The thought of abandonment was so intense that I could think of nothing else. Things felt like they were going too well for me; surely the peace was transitory, I feared.

My fears, unfortunately, were not completely unfounded.

Jay's mental health began to decline further, and he expressed his fervent desire to jump into our sedan and steer himself into a bluff at blinding speed. Perhaps Joe, this source of solace for me, could save the life of my husband. Perchance he was mighty enough to prevent a suicide. I encouraged Jay to contact Joe to set up an appointment.

Jay wrote, "Hi! I would like to know what appointment times may be available for myself over the next few weeks. Thank you!"

Joe's unforeseen response:

"Hi Jay,

Thanks for reaching out. Unfortunately, as I work with Allison, I would be unable to see you as well given ethical concerns … "

And he proceeded to express that a "Dr. David Sacks," whom Joe knows "personally and professionally," takes Aetna Insurance, and that he is "outstanding."

Choking back tears at Joe's response, I actually considered relinquishing my spot so that Jay could have it. I hadn't realized that therapists don't often see family members, and I didn't know if anyone in the world could be as effective as Joe. Unbeknownst to me at the time, David would be the hero of the saga.

David agreed to counsel both of us for the issues intrinsic to Jay's suffering. It became immediately clear that Joe was accurate about David's remarkable insightfulness and benevolence.

Summer began to peek through the blustery spring, and the heat of the sun echoed the warmth illuminating my healing soul. One Friday, I ambled into my individual therapy appointment with Joe, knowing that he would be strong enough to help me fight the week's challenges. With some hesitation, I spilled to him that I had indeed seen a real reduction in anxiety levels since treatment, but that I was embarrassed to perceive him as a liberator, and for those of you who may be *Boy Meets World* fans, as the "Mr. Feeny" in my life that I had always hoped for. (I knew this was illogical, because my psychologist was far from the persona of a legendary old man who strangely taught English and life lessons to the same beloved students in every single grade through their childhood.) Joe laughed and declared that he also highly esteemed *Boy Meets World* ... Then his voice wavered and slowed, and in a peculiar tone bluntly spoke:

"I am actually a VERY old man."

I was perplexed, but moved on.

"So how do I prevent myself from being forced to engage in some sort of wild chair throwing frenzy in your office?"

Joe seemed stupefied but recovered and adeptly began to explore some of the reasons for my distress.

"Do you think there's any way that your judgments about yourself could be playing into this?"

Embarrassed, I began to weep, eventually strengthening myself to peek up at his face. There he sat, stone faced and awaiting my gaze. The session concluded too soon.

He told me that I might feel a little bit raw for a while.

Chapter 10

$$\begin{vmatrix} 1 & 0 & 0 \\ 0 & 1 & 0 \\ 0 & 0 & 1 \end{vmatrix}$$

TRAGEDY

If there were any section of life to which I could turn back the hands of time, this is undeniably the era I would choose. 1:04 pm on Friday, May 31 is eternally seared in my memory.

Whispering in the lobby of our new psychologist, David, we awaited our appointment. Right on the hour, David welcomed us as usual. Jay and I promenaded into his office, sat down in our customary spots, and waited for guidance. David gazed directly at me and asked how my individual sessions had been going with Joe. Interesting question to start with .... Relaxed and enthusiastic, I noted how extraordinarily it had been going.

He spoke slowly and steadily, "I'm afraid I have some news about Joe."

I began to writhe internally, as concern and confusion enshrouded. Perhaps I was right. Perhaps Joe had decided that I was exasperating and was through with helping me, but had asked his psychologist buddy, David, to break the news to me.

But David continued. "Last weekend, Joe passed away."

My world melted like wax. I waned into that liquefying world and just wept, clutching onto my husband beside me, stopping occasionally to muster a question. I eyed the floor and considered throwing myself upon it and wailing with abandon.

How can this be? Joe was a very young individual, 32 years old, not chronically ill, and gone suddenly. What was the cause of death? He had made that bizarre claim to be old ...

I had had a dream the night before I found out about Joe. I sorely wished I had told it to David prior to finding out about the tragedy. In the dream, I was visiting an ethereal tower, in which Joe resided. His room somewhat resembled his therapy office, but curiously, I was not invited all the way inside to sit in the client chair. Instead, I resolved to hover near the entrance. Joe was also standing and gracefully handed me an exam (a therapy exam of sorts), which boasted a grade of 97% at the top. With dismay I eyed him— happy for the A, but yearning for a 100. "I'm so sorry. If I had known, I would have worked harder," I blubbered to him. He smiled and gently shook his head. "You did an excellent job," he slowly uttered. The camera lens of the dream then shifted to reveal the happenings of first floor of this tower, where my departed grandparents feasted around a munificent table. Suddenly compelled to gaze out a window, I witnessed the explosion of something akin to a space shuttle, lighting up the sky in bewildering pandemonium. I wondered in the dream whether something tragic was impending.

I began to replay all of the last things I remember Joe doing prior to his death. With terror, I recalled that I was quite sure I had seen Joe the day that he died. It was Friday afternoon, and he had been heading south near his office. Jay and I had been driving north after having been out to eat, and we had passed a noteworthy car heading in the opposite direction. That driver was Joe. I saw Joe's face and that memorable sideways head movement, but he looked irate. His mouth was open like he was shouting, which alarmed me. He had always been this docile, serene being, but here he was, appearing inconsolable while careening down Highway 100. I counseled myself that therapists have problems, too, and that possibly he wasn't enraged at all, but instead was reveling in heavy metal music. Either way, I considered texting him. I surely couldn't pose a question about his own mental health, but I could express gratitude for his help. I did not send that text. I just failed to send that text.

Intense grief about this tragic death replaced the warmth in my soul. I was powerless to do anything but ponder the way Joe was feeling upon dying and how traumatized Joe's family must be. Imagining ever being happy again became incomprehensible. What is the point of being happy when you can't trust that your family and friends will even make it through the day? What is the point of planning for the future? People say that it's ridiculous to ignore budgets and 10-year financial plans and that you should responsibly eat beans and rice while working to get rich slowly, but in grief, it feels more sensible to live recklessly. Why not try to live the life that I want to live, given the uncertainty of life?

Joe was clearly gifted, bright, and slayed darkness with his illumination prowess. It is senseless that Joe would be gone. Perhaps therapy is fickle and untrustworthy, I reasoned. To climb a mountain may be rewarding and majestic, but to fall from that height is cataclysmic.

I had told Joe one day that I needed help with my "carpe-diem-way-too-hard" compulsions. People constantly talk about life being fragile and precious and to savor every good moment, but I have always taken this to the extreme, because I have always been genuinely surprised and relieved to have made it through the day. When every day dawns with the view of assailants, it feels like a miracle to just endure. But alas, the person who was helping me to live outside of a state of hyper-vigilance was gone, and was the same age as my husband and myself. How then was I supposed to live?

It was a suicide.

Posts on Facebook were rampant, and mental health was a keyword in posts about Joe. This death of Joe was by suicide. He had willfully chosen to abandon his post. Given the OCD fears I have battled of death via going crazy and committing suicide, my mind became swarmed with a whirlwind of competing thoughts: belief in the strategies that Joe taught me on the one hand, and the hideous thoughts that had previously plagued me on the other, as if the "OCD" thoughts enlivened in sadistic awareness of the departure of my brain coach (Joe).

I was powerless to disconnect Joe's face, as last viewed, from my mind. There was never a time in my life in which I felt so much palpable compassion and security as when sitting in that office during therapy. But the ending was a sour demonstration of the fragility of life, of how trustworthiness may be a childish fantasy.

Joe was an exemplary psychologist, and not a day proceeded that I did not lament about my inability to prevent this tragedy. I have no reason to believe I had the skills to do so, but nevertheless, I mourned that I hadn't discerned just a bit better. Once again, during the last session, I had thanked Joe for being that Mr. Feeny. I also had expressed gratitude to Joe for having helped me through a challenging time working a part-time job to pay off some bills. I had cheered to Joe,

"I am so thrilled; the job is almost over, and then I get to go to the good place." (meaning my regular university teaching job).

Joe, usually decorous in demeanor, briefly lost it in a fitful laugh, *"AHAHA- 'the good place'—it sounds like you're like going to heaven."* In this session, Joe also mentioned soon being able to "finally go on vacation."

In addition, I had tried to ask Joe for guidance about how often I should schedule appointments for the future, in terms of my progress, and Joe would not really address this question. The conversation went like this:

Me: "What would be the best amount of time between sessions?"

Joe: "It's really whatever you prefer."

Me: "What is your suggestion?"

Joe: "You are really smart and can figure things out, so it really doesn't matter for you."

Once in an earlier session, I had been philosophizing about the rapid but sometimes capricious speed at which time progresses, and how it was maddeningly inexorable. I also mentioned that sometimes I just wonder, being no longer a very young adult, if I made the correct choices in life:

"Do you ever wonder if you made the correct life choice?"

Joe: pause ... pause ... pause ... "Every Day."

It truly isn't a bizarre sentiment to express in everyday life, but in hindsight, the memory of his intonation and facial expression is chilling.

To Joe: I cannot fathom how and why this unthinkable tragedy occurred, but there are no words powerful enough to express my gratitude for your having started my process of healing. You gave me hope that I had never known, and insight that I did not know could exist in the world. Thank you for sending me to David, whom you very well knew is uniquely strong enough to help me. I hold onto hope that I will be able to express that to you one day in "the good place."

Chapter 11

$$\begin{vmatrix} 1 & 0 & 0 \\ 0 & 1 & 0 \\ 0 & 0 & 1 \end{vmatrix}$$

TO TRUST AGAIN?

Did I still need individual therapy? Should I thrust myself into trusting in it once again? These were the brash, pressing thoughts interjecting themselves between my grieving gasps. Intellectually, it seemed like I should try. To coerce myself to do so, I began to evoke the comparison game. What are the similarities and differences of my psychologists? Could David help me like Joe did? Perhaps he could help me even more? After all, this had assuredly been Joe's wish.

The Similarities

- Deep Compassion

- Impressive Intelligence

- Profound Insight

- Similar Office set up—psychologist closer to door—presumably for ease of escape in case of thrashing lunatic client?

- Well-stocked supply of tissues for said lunatic client

- Stylish, expensive looking furniture

- Austere Desk area

- Room smells like a guy (not malodourous at all—a nice smell kind of like mouthwash)

- Those brown shoes! They wore the same shoes! Apparently, I had spent a lot of time avoiding eye contact and staring at feet, because I am the last person in the world to care about shoes. With little exception, I wear the same pair until they completely disintegrate. But like those unique moments when you walk outside and the warmth of the sun strikes you just right such that all feels well with the world, and you bask in the warmth of being alive, those chocolate shoes are oddly consoling.

The Differences

- Joe had a plethora of books in his office; David has just a few.

- Joe's deep bellowing laughs vs. David's quieter laugh

- David always seems so motivated to start sessions. Near the end of working with Joe, he would appear to have to psyche himself up to start a session. David's demeanor fluctuates less.

- PERPETUAL HOMEWORK PASS! DAVID DOESN'T ASK ME TO DO WRITTEN WORK. *Actually Joe only did one time, and then he wasn't there to receive my homework assignment.*

- Besides the books, Joe's office was more unadorned. But Joe had a massive sunlit window, and there is no outside facing window in David's office.

- David never seems tired.

Chapter 12

$$\begin{vmatrix} 1 & 0 & 0 \\ 0 & 1 & 0 \\ 0 & 0 & 1 \end{vmatrix}$$

THE PSYCHIATRISTS

Nearly six months had passed, and David's healing guidance was revealed in the process. In discussing some of my deranged tales, I contemplated seeking psychiatric help as well. I hadn't been to a psychiatrist since the great panic of 2009, and I have great trepidation about taking any medications, having abandoned Xanax and Lexapro back in 2009/2010. Even when I decide to take Tylenol, I generally take the child dose, in fear of toxicity. I also usually ask my husband to administer medicine to me, fearing that I may accidentally take the whole bottle without realizing it.

So I called around halfheartedly, being told often that the psychiatrists were not accepting new patients. No problems there—I didn't really want a psychiatrist ... too terrified of pills. Because my husband seemed very passionate about my finding someone, I kept calling. Eventually, one office announced that their psychiatrist was accepting new patients. It was an odd encounter, and transpired as follows:

Me: "Hi! Are you accepting new patients?"

Receptionist: "Yes, our doctor is. Tell me about your diagnosis."

Me: "Well I have a diagnosis of OCD."

Receptionist: "Oh ... Well he doesn't really treat that. Do you have any other diagnoses?"

I felt confused at this point, shuffling in my head for other disorders that he might treat. I didn't want psychiatric care anyhow, but I also didn't adore the feeling of being rejected on account of my apparently obtrusive diagnosis.

Me: "Well I am pretty anxious... "

Receptionist: "Thank you for the information. I will present this to him, and we will give you a call back in the next few days to let you know whether or not you have been accepted for a first appointment. Just so that you are aware, if you are granted a first appointment, that doesn't guarantee you additional appointments."

Terrifying!

But I got the call three days later that I had been approved for a first appointment. So I waited a week for this appointment, during which time additional phone calls from this intriguing group provoked further confusion:

Same Receptionist: "Hi. I just wanted to let you know that there was a cancellation for tomorrow, so do you want to come early?"

Me: "What time is the appointment?"

Receptionist: "10:30."

Me: "I teach a class at that time, but thank you."

Receptionist: "No problem. See you next Thursday at 9 am."

Two hours went by. I was working on grading in my office. The phone rang again:

Same Receptionist: "Hi! We had a cancellation for tomorrow. Would you like to come to an earlier appointment?"

Me: "Is this the same appointment that is at 10:30?"

Receptionist: "Yes. I guess I had already called you?"

I reasoned that perhaps they were trying to test me for how off my rocker I was. I received two more duplicate calls (about the location) prior to the appointment.

On the day of arrival for that appointment, I was intensely anxious. It had been 10 years since my last jamboree with a psychiatrist; maybe the first had missed something ominous about my brain. I awakened at 3:45 am and just waited in terror until the time in which I would have to drive there. I arrived nearly an hour early and went in to sign papers. Below the standard health questionnaire was printed something alarming. I was required to sign a statement affirming that even if accepted as a patient, if I ever were hospitalized or felt suicidal, I would no longer be allowed to be treated by this psychiatrist.

Again. Terrifying! But I had never been hospitalized, and I could certainly keep the past suicidal worries on the downlow.

Eventually I was ushered into a second waiting room, one without windows, but consisting of three mystery doors and some enchanting 3-D flower artwork adorning the pale walls. Resounding at the base of one of those doors was a noise cancellation device, so I reasoned that this was his office. At about 8 minutes past the hour, a joyful lady sauntered out of his office. The door from which she exited then slammed behind her, and then approximately 10 seconds later, the psychiatrist emerged. It seemed as if he had just been hovering behind the door, breathing slowly to rest for a spell, and counting to 10 before having to don his gleeful face once again. It was impressive that he felt capable of having so little time between patients. He literally bounced out of his office, extending his hand with a cordial greeting and spirited zest. Incredulousness and comfort intermittently swirled through me. Massive windows welcomed my entrance into his stunning office, cascading light upon the tastefully ornamented walls and lavish sofas. He began with the warning that I had become accustomed to with this bunch.

"Just to let you know, I am a different kind of psychiatrist. I spend a lot of time with my patients, and I don't think it's fair to agree to treat someone with a condition outside of my wheelhouse."

Fair enough.

As we faced each other, each scrutinizing the other, the session commenced. He began with a boring question, posing first what issues I had been dealing with most recently. I began by relaying the information about my deceased therapist and a recent death of a student and that I struggled with anxiety. I inspected his face for signs of his comfort with my "condition." It felt more like a job interview than a doctor's appointment. I had planned to start with these situational disturbances as a way to perhaps convince him that I am not in fact crazy, and also to make him realize I wouldn't be a suitable candidate for abandonment.

He seemed to be comfortable with my stories, so I relaxed. I hadn't yet been ejected. It was time to begin discussing my history. I explained that the incidence of significant tormenting symptoms had been at age 8. I expounded that it started out as mostly hypochondria, but I also seemed to worry more than others about the world conspiring against me, wondering if people would at some point peel the masks off of their faces and reveal their monstrous identities. I even made sure that I qualified that statement with something like "I know that sounds crazy, though."

It didn't work. His face froze, and he reclined slightly with stiffening shoulders.

Psychiatrist: "So I am not going to be the right provider for you, as I can't rule out psychosis."

Seriously? Psychosis?! I choked back perturbed tears. To make matters worse, he told me that he wouldn't be charging me, and he escorted me out a back door so that I wouldn't re-emerge in the main office. My family later told me that this was kind for him to not charge me. I can see that. He was gentle in general, but to be told by a physician that you will not even be charged implies that you are so far off the scale that it would aggravate their conscience to grab money from such a pathetic soul.

That psychiatrist declared that I needed a more comprehensive psychiatric facility. So I made an appointment at an outpatient facility that has a psychiatric hospital attached. I assumed that my problems were not too convoluted for them. Due to the appointment being six weeks in the future at the time of scheduling, I decided to find another provider who may perhaps be available sooner.

It was a week before Christmas, so it would probably be tough to find anyone with availability. But one practitioner was indeed available—someone who looked particularly friendly, like she may have cookies and milk or goody-bags for patients as they depart. *(For some reason, the more docile looking the psychiatrist, the better. The opposite is true for my preference of therapist. David is particularly herculean/ninja-seeming, and I am comforted by that, because I'm always worried about random people storming in and attacking, and he looks like he could ward off such an invader. But I would prefer for my <u>psychiatrist</u> to be somewhat old, lanky, and slow, someone from whom I could most easily escape ... as if people often find themselves sprinting ill-fatedly from crazed assailing psychiatrists.)*

The phone conversation was swell: (I spoke directly to the psychiatrist, as she has a private practice and covers her own calls.)

"How may I help you?" she spouted with marked enthusiasm and the sweetest voice of a cookie-toting grandmother.

"I have been having a difficult time and am wondering what your availability is like right now."

"I have some openings after New Year's."

"Do you have anything available sooner? I have to teach again starting the first full week of January, and if I were to even consider taking any medication, it would be very helpful to try it out prior to having to go back to work."

"I could actually do the morning of December 26th."

I liked her. I thought to myself that certainly I could tell her my problems (some of them), and from her picture and the sound of her voice, I could easily outrun her, if necessary.

But I noticed something shocking and horrifying about her profile. It looked like her office address was similar to where Joe's office had been. In astonishment, I tried to recall exactly what the address had been for Joe and quickly determined that she was indeed in the same building. Could I even consider revisiting that building, a fortress that once offered freedom and hope and now undoubtedly had sunk in a mire of death and defeat? I quickly sent the affable psychiatrist an email and asked for another brief phone conversation, to which she conceded the following day.

I probably sounded very strange, grilling her on exactly where her office was in the building, what it was near, whose office was adjacent...

Psychiatrist: stated slowly with an air of bewilderment: *"Is that a problem?"*

I hesitated, unsure if what I was going to say would come out intelligibly.

I squeaked, *"Actually, I was asking because I'm pretty sure my former therapist was in your building and he killed himself, and I don't know whether I can handle being there."*

Psychiatrist: first silence and then a slow response, *"Oh. This hasn't happened to me before. Yes; we were told that we got this office because of a suicide."*

So there it was. If I wanted to get this psychiatry thing over with quickly, I would have to revisit not only Joe's old building, but his exact office ... and sit there watching the sweet lady resting where Joe would sit, where he would turn his head ever so slightly and guffaw, where he would take notes solemnly and then try to make me feel like he didn't think I was crazy by asking, "Do you think that I'm sitting here thinking *HOLY SH*T, this one's crazy!?"*

The day after Christmas came, and it had been a tumultuous few days. Unfortunately, I was under tremendous torment yet again. I couldn't slay the suicidal obsession which Joe's death had fanned. Luckily, I had therapy the day after this new psychiatry appointment, a phenomenal safety net in case the appointment was tremendously psychologically injurious to me.

Pulling up to Joe's former building felt like driving down a gravel road into fog on the way to a graveyard. Entering the office building was like visiting a ghost town. The building had deteriorated remarkably in his absence. I noticed every defect. Dangling at a menacing angle, the ceiling tiles appeared to sneer at me, and their stains had spread, almost continuing to do so as I watched, brown mysterious malevolent substances oozing out of the cracks. The walls weren't the friendly colors that I remembered, but looked sort of haphazardly painted such that the edges near the floor and ceiling were grimy junctions unfitting for a professional establishment. Miserable was the state of the couches that lined the upstairs offices; they had become decrepit and lopsided, and looked like they had been picked up from the side of the road. The building reeked of decaying plant matter and the lights flickered threateningly, seemingly dimming with each additional step down the hall.

Had my husband not been with me, I would have split, and perhaps worn garlic around my neck for a week. But there she was, the warm and welcoming woman from the photo. As we approached her, she informed us, intent on catching my reaction, that she had been unable to procure a different office and hoped that this would be ok. My husband jumped in to save me, my protector.

Husband: "She really can't handle being in that office. Is there anywhere else at all where we could meet?"

God bless him, I was unable to speak at that moment.

Psychiatrist: "Well there is this conference room here. But it doesn't have a window, so we have to use the awful fluorescent lights."

I found my voice.

Me: "Yes, please! I hate fluorescent lights, too, and I know Joe had an awesome window, but I just can't handle it."

So we met in the conference room. As an athlete, I felt as though I knew how to handle nervousness, but I was so overcome with panic that I could barely utter a coherent word. Trying to extinguish the butterflies, I rocked awkwardly backward and forward, alternating between placing my head gently on the desk to stretching backwards in my chair, all the while clenching my hands or pinching my thighs in feeble attempt to distract myself from the incessant torture ... for ... the ... whole ... hour ... and ... 15 minutes.

How did I explain a lifetime of torture in that amount of time? I basically just described how I had felt tormented my entire life. That at the worst points, I have felt as though my consciousness, the essence of me, was eroding and seeping down through the lower portion of my body and into my surroundings until I could no longer sense that I existed ... or exactly where I was. Generally the feelings would alternate, I explained, between that eroded essence of existence, and thinking that I had some unusual disease. I also tried to talk up the OCD symptoms. Yes, I had always gone back 14 times to check to see whether the oven was off, and would sometimes do odd things like slink back into my office to touch my right hand on the desk if the left one hit it on the way out (because somehow the unevenness felt like it would cause some great calamity to occur). Afterwards came the questions that scared me the most. Did I ever see things that others couldn't? Very rarely. Do I hear voices? This was something that had been brought to my attention recently. Everyone knows that you just do not agree to hearing voices, because in my layman's view, that is the quintessential indicator of genuine craziness. As my husband has been diagnosed as well with OCD, I asked him whether or not he ever felt like internal (clearly not perceived like actual voices) scary sounding voices commanded him to do things, lest he or someone else would die. Surprisingly, he denied ever hearing such voices. I had thought that this was a normal human experience.

So back to her question:

Psychiatrist: "Do you ever hear voices?"

Me: "Not like you and I are talking. I have perceptions of a monstrous voice from inside of my head commanding me to do the compulsive things that I do to prevent something terrible from occurring ... but I know that sounds crazy ... and again, it's not something I hear with my ears."

Psychiatrist: "How often?"

Me: "I don't know. Every other day?"

The rest of the session continued, and I seemed to wear out the adrenaline response, slightly improving in ability to maintain a straightforward gaze.

The sentencing period was impending, and I braced myself. She set down her clipboard and said, *"Well, you are very interesting! You clearly have OCD, but seem to also fall somewhere on the psychotic spectrum."*

There was that word again. Distressingly, she professed her suggestion that I should take a low dose of an antipsychotic drug instead of the antidepressant that I had been expecting. Absolutely not! But as to not be disrespectful, I told her I would consider it and quickly changed the subject to asking about how her holiday went.

The session ended with my husband standing up and thanking her, also spouting with a grin, *"She was afraid you would lock her up,"* to which she turned to me with a demanding stare, *"Do you have suicidal thoughts?"*

"No!" I lied. She seemed like the type who clearly wouldn't hesitate to make that phone call. I would drive to the hospital if I truly couldn't handle it anymore ... certainly wouldn't allow some other person to do it for me.

Chapter 13

$$\begin{vmatrix} 1 & 0 & 0 \\ 0 & 1 & 0 \\ 0 & 0 & 1 \end{vmatrix}$$

MY DIAGNOSIS CRAZE

What's in a name, and more importantly, what's in a diagnosis? During that last psychiatry appointment, I was asked whether or not I had ever done any written tests for mental illness. I didn't divulge, but I actually had taken the MMPI2 exam (the Minnesota Multiphasic Personality Inventory, which is apparently a diagnostic tool). It is a lengthy exam with 500+ True/False questions. I have included some of my results in the following table. Joe seemed to have liked the exam, as his dissertation had heavily focused upon it. Would the test pin me as crazy? A Bamboozler? A Whiner?

Index	Raw Score	T-Score
VRIN	7	58
TRIN	9	50
F	12	79
Fb	12	89
Fp	6	89
L	7	66
K	7	32
S	13	35
Hypochondriasis	8	46
Depression	22	53
Hysteria	25	56
Psychopathic Deviate	22	55
Paranoia	11	52
Psychasthenia	29	66
Schizophrenia	35	75
Hypomania	20	53
Introversion	44	68

My discussion of the preceding table was informed by a PsychCentral.com website[1] and includes my slipshod, "C+ in Psychology 101" interpretations.

T-scores (third column) – Scores between 40 and 60 describe most of the population:

> *"50" would be average, the peak of a Gaussian (normal) curve, with a standard deviation of 10. So a score above 70 would be 2 standard deviations away from the mean and would thus have a probability of 2.28%.*

Raw Scores (second column) These are just sums of questions that were answered in such a way as to indicate that the test taker may have whatever condition is shown. Higher is usually bad.

VRIN (Variable Response Inconsistency) – For example, they ask you multiple times if you love your parents. It is assumed that you haven't changed your mind by the middle of the test...

TRIN (True Response Inconsistency) – Answering "True" too many times, like you got hopelessly bored during the interminable exam and stopped paying attention...

F – A high score indicates distress. (Above 70 indicates mental illness.) Mine is upsettingly high.

Fb – The test is incredibly long! They basically give you a second F score for the second half to see if you appear the same level of disturbed throughout the whole thing.

Fp – This is supposed to test whether you are faking a mental illness. If the T-score is above 100, it seems to be highly suggestive of the test-taker feigning illness.

L – Lie! This tests for how much I have tried to make myself look like a good, moral person!

K – This is a defensiveness test, and apparently higher scores correlate with education levels! Mine being low apparently means I have low "ego strength" or am a mythomaniac.

S – This correlates with the K scale and also can confirm whether someone appears well-adjusted and confident.

Hypochondriasis – Fear of having illnesses ... and mine is normal!?!? But then again, I am not sure that the questions related to hypochondria were well adapted to my oddities. For instance, I recall questions that went something like "I go to the doctor often." However, I avoid doctors for fear of there actually being something wrong with me ... So False! ... Other questions are sort of like "There is something wrong with my health." Of course, I would have to answer false for fear of claiming true and cursing myself.

Depression – Mine looks normal! I don't normally feel the strong feelings of guilt that the test seemed to value.

Hysteria – Apparently this relates to your level of neuroticism. The test hilariously deems me not neurotic...

Psychopathic Deviate – Lack of enjoyable life occurrences and social problems ... All good here as well, somehow...

Paranoia – I made sure to avoid answering "True" to any of the overtly paranoid sounding questions (people are out to get me type notions), and clearly succeeded in not being considered paranoid.

Psychasthenia – I had certainly never heard this word before … Evidently it tests for OCD-like thoughts. Mine is sort of high, but not above 70! I have no idea what kept my score low here. I recall questions about avoiding sidewalk cracks and such and assuredly marked "True" for those...

Schizophrenia – My score on this one was the highest, which horrified me upon first impression. But evidently the test doesn't diagnose the disease very well, although it can confirm the existence of peculiar thought patterns.

Hypomania – Some questions seemed to center around racing thoughts and shaky hands, which I denied. I didn't really understand the concept of a racing thought … When the tormenting thoughts have harassed me, they spoke at reasonable tempos. How fast do they have to speak to be considered racing? And my hands haven't shaken often … the rest of my body has, but not really my hands. Normal Score.

Introversion – Sure. I would prefer to drift along a tranquil lagoon than navigate some chaotic party.

$

Who cares? I did. I thought perhaps a firmer diagnosis would provide a path out of the cerebral thickets.

$$\oint$$

Back to psychiatry, take 3. The sweet psychiatrist was wonderful, but she didn't take my insurance. The psychiatric hospital, where the third psychiatrist of this narrative exists, is a fearsome place. You aren't permitted to use the stairs to go up to the third floor, and the elevator will not stop on the second floor without a key. I have no idea what occurs on the second floor, but I know that I never want to find out. When you arrive on the third floor, there are few windows and a dimly lit labyrinth of hallways leading seemingly nowhere, with the occasional waiting room, where perturbed looking people sit frozen in anticipation of their appointment.

I wondered what jarring discussions may transpire during my new psychiatry appointments. I recall going to one of the follow-up appointments 10 years ago during that shadowy era, and suddenly the psychiatrist puffed up in anticipation to ask his fundamental question:

Psychiatrist: "I don't know if you'll be comfortable with my asking this question with <u>HER</u> in the room with you. But does the Lexapro cause you any sexual side effects?"

The "HER" was actually spoken at 50 decibels higher than the other words in the sentence, with a clear accompanying growl and strange sideways glance toward my bemused stepmom.

I always found that odd. Anyway, during mental health appointments in general (both psychiatry and psychology), my husband habitually would divulge his darkest feelings and chronic debilitating pain and then sort of recoil and express that perhaps he was just making everything up. The stark contrast between the response of our psychologist and psychiatrist to his "What if I'm just making everything up" was somewhat hilarious. David adeptly would proceed to explore the thought more deeply, never seeming surprised or flustered. The psychiatrist would look befuddled and spout "What!?!?"

I had a month to pregame for this psychiatry appointment. I sort of wanted to rehearse to make sure that I come across as just having OCD and not something unknown and sinister. Although I truly did want to know: What was wrong with me?! Perhaps if a diagnosis fit perfectly, I could find others who would understand me. I had briefly read what I could find on the different disorders online, and I didn't seem to fit well into any of them. Don't mistake my definitions/explanations of the disorders, below, for what is actually scientifically valid...

Was I depressed?

 I have seen depression ravage my husband's mind and mercilessly pilfer his youth. He would lie in bed from dawn until dusk, failing to even eat as his frail body did not allow him the strength to shuffle to the kitchen for a morsel of food. He had a sense of utter hopelessness, felt there was no purpose in living a futile life, that he was unworthy of love, a "free-loader" as he erroneously calls himself. I would come home from work daily with the gnawing fear about what I would find when I returned home. Would he still be alive? The sheer hopelessness is ruthless. This penetrating lack of motivation is not something I have directly experienced. Of course, I have frequently battled intense suicidal-feeling turmoil, but it always was accompanied by intense panic that drove me to pace the house, clawing at my legs and face, in futile attempt to ground myself, to feel something real. You know, they often give you depression screening quizzes at doctor appointments, and on those there is always that question about whether or not you are feeling suicidal. Definitely in those periods of time in which I battled that incessantly, I would never have admitted to it on one of those quizzes. Perhaps others would, but I certainly would not have done so. I began considering what type of question could lead someone to know that I was in dire need of help.

For me, any of these would have worked to clue someone in to the suicidal ideation:

1. Is consciousness difficult to maintain? (Although involuntary, even breathing and perceiving seemed like manual labor.)
2. How tiring is consciousness? (Just existing felt like extreme work.)
3. Why isn't the suicide rate higher than it already is? (In the depths of despair, I was inclined to

respond that I am surprised by everyone else in the world's desire to thrive.)

4. Without looking at a clock, how long do you think this appointment has run? (How does my perception of time compare to reality?)

Am I a typical Generalized Anxiety Disorder/ Panic Disorder patient?

I know of these terms, because they line the top of my medical charts. I am always the lunatic of the day when I go to non-psychiatric medical appointments, and they always throw those terms at me as I rock back and forth and clutch my stomach in childlike terror from the fear of visiting a doctor. I even get nervous talking to my own father, who is a physician, about any health concerns. The stigma has lifted a bit for anxiety disorders. Everyone knows what fear and anxiety and stress feel like. Perhaps most people do not have a diagnosable anxiety disorder, but I would imagine that the rate is not all that low. I think that I could say that I have an anxiety disorder in the work setting, and no one would bat an eye. I wouldn't, of course, but even in an interview setting, I feel that I could perhaps divulge this without being initially shunned, but I probably couldn't explain why I used to think I was amorphous like a worm … In the interview setting, the question that would likely follow a conversation about anxiety would be how I manage stress in difficult times, and if answered correctly, I could even earn extra points. Anxiety disorders feel awful, like you're getting electrocuted while being chased by a demented hyena all day long, but they aren't completely unrelatable.

Obsessive Compulsive Disorder (OCD)?

I stood in front of the chalkboard, drawing an example general linear model on the board, but I needed more space. So I grabbed the eraser and began to erase some prior distribution I had messily sketched on the board. I paused. The remnant chalk pattern didn't look right … didn't feel right … so I erased it further, blending the lines in a more appealing way. A student jeered:

"You are so totally OCD."

I tarried with my back turned to him, eraser still pressed against the board, trying to formulate a response …

Generally everyone agrees on this diagnosis for me. It doesn't sound all that crazy. People often use the expression in jest "I am so OCD about … " Having OCD is like being trapped your entire life with relentless piranha-like thoughts that sabotage your sanity. So it's just easier to give in to the urges to go back and touch your left arm on the wall where your right arm just grazed, because life would just feel slightly more "right." I know that other people with diagnosed OCD also check the stove 74 times per day to make sure it is actually off and double and triple check that the doors are locked to obstruct impending intruders. Most people have had some experience with multiple checking compulsions. (Have you ever had a super important exam or interview or flight early in the morning and feel compelled to check your cell phone alarm 20 times to make sure that you actually set it before collapsing into sleep?) But with OCD, such things never leave. There is never a day, never a moment when you are offered a reprieve from these compulsions about everything. You will never stop, never rest until you are 100% sure that everything will be alright. Because it is generally accepted that no one can be 100% certain, there really is never an incentive to stop worrying. Have you ever accidentally turned onto a road at night going the wrong way? Suddenly, you're gripped by a perplexed, perturbed feeling. Something feels off, wickedly so, but you're initially confused as to what. Clues begin to stream in to imply that you've made an error, most noteworthy of which include oncoming headlights until you gracefully mount and dismount the center median to get back on track. That mental median is mischievously hard to find without therapy, so being stuck in an OCD crisis feels more like fighting to just dodge the oncoming cars.

It also feels like a ghoulish version of the game Apples to Apples. I love the regular version of this game: In the game, every player is dealt five cards with a noun written on each card. In each round, one player is the judge and selects a card with an adjective written on it from a pile, after which the other players choose which one of their five cards best fits that adjective, and hand it to the judge. The point of the game is to debate with each other about which noun card best exemplifies the adjective written on the card of the judge of the round. In each round, the judge rotates. Example: The judge draws an adjective such as "Aloof!" Then the other players look through their cards and draw the one they think they can best argue is the most aloof. The winner of the round, as adjudicated by the judge, earns the adjective card and thus gleans a point, so the room of play fills with the joyous sound of a family debating whether clothespins or lobsters are more aloof. This the blithe version of the game.

In the OCD version of the game, there are internal voices perpetually shouting and arguing for their side to be believed about a disconcerting matter, such as the reason for carrying on in a dismal world. The typical judge adjective card is swapped out for a noun like "me" or "reality." Then invisible, evil participants of unknown quantity slam down adjective cards that they argue are the most like me, or about reality of the world. Some argue for *delusional*, boasting deranged examples. Others contend for weak, insipid, sick, depressed, unworthy, unreal, robotic, moronic, etc ... But prior to their onslaught, I am permitted to concoct arguments to support myself or reality, and must, in expectation of the attack to come, circulate through all possible accusations that they may bring, and formulate arguments against their future claims. Unfortunately, in presenting their dismal adjectives and justifications, there always has seemed to be a miserably good point brought up, something that doesn't quite make logical sense but strikes my mind as being close to doing so, such that I am entranced by it and must descend into that pit of consternation to logically battle that semi-logical, gilded thought accusation and convince the mysterious judge of the round that I am the correct player, the winner. If my argument prevailed not, then must I concede and believe the claims of the evil players inside my head?

Sometimes in playing the normal game, you have the perfect card. Sure, the judge may choose to be malicious and pick a different winner, but nonetheless, you know that your card will be the most logical regardless of what else is thrown down. For example: if the adjective is terrifying and your card reads "torture," then you assuredly have a winner. In all likelihood, the other cards will read something like "socks," "bananas," and "twisty straws," and they will have no chance. But what if the judge's word is something difficult, related to why we will never go crazy and go around punching random people or harming ourselves? There is confusion; does anyone know what keeps them from this? So there is no card that could possibly yield that beautiful ahhhhh feeling of the perfect answer, and assuredly the screaming head opponents may offer confusing answers, casting doubt on your control over your own actions, internal beliefs, and reality.

More specifically, it feels as though my brain and I are separate dueling entities. A thought comes across about how I know that I can prevent myself from harming myself in such a way as Joe did, and I just know that soon there will be several other internal agents in my brain debating with my brain to go with them and believe that self-harm would be worth it. It feels like my only hope of not succumbing to that would be to contrive an argument to my brain that will be superior to those other opponents, and to keep shouting my analytically rational points, lest my brain be magnetically drawn to those arguments of my assailants against my will.

The "Psychotic Spectrum"

When I had gone to that brief psychiatric appointment at age 22, my sense of existence sinking from my face down through my legs until I felt I couldn't distinguish myself from the walls and the floor, the psychiatrist declared that he didn't think I was going crazy, because I was so freaked out by my symptoms. I had mentioned earlier that perhaps it sounds unusual to have internal commanding voices, but somehow they have never been permitted to overtake me. I indeed have always done things like throw out water bottles if I have left them unattended in my office or car, as I have perceived that something or someone may desire to poison me. I suppose I can agree that this sounds paranoid. Further, I do things like if I'm listening to a song and the word "death" is sung and I happen to be looking at my food or beverage while this happens, feel that the word has contaminated my food or beverage and I have to throw it out, lest I get sick consuming it.

$$\oint$$

The day of the third psychiatry appointment had arrived. Checking into the establishment, the individual behind me was another faculty member that I knew. It is a unique feeling to observe a colleague in such an inauspicious place. We exchanged empathetic looks and chatted in the waiting room for about 20 minutes. One thing working in my favor for this appointment, in terms of wanting so badly to look sane, was that I had often accompanied my husband to this same appointment and had always appeared, in my view, fairly ordinary. I had always been the lucid one of the couple. I knew the drill—the resident physician greets us and ushers us into this dungeon-like office with a blacked out window which we imagined doctors examining us from behind. The resident interrogates, after which she conveys her medication judgement, and departs to summon the attending physician, who bustles in and basically asks for you to repeat things. Afterward, he generally verbally harmonizes with the resident, and then smiles and farewells ensue. This was not so different. I explained my current struggles, the past experiences of just completely losing it, and she began reassuring me that she didn't think I was, or had ever been, psychotic, just severely obsessive. So the consensus from this appointment was this was very extreme OCD and that they assumed an SSRI would help. These psychiatrists are exceptional and seem to have a true knack for personalizing their assessments and asserting what will work for each individual. My husband's concoction of medicines under their care has been instrumental in bringing him peace.

Diagnosis Incredulity

Unexpectedly, 1 lost concern about my specific diagnosis. When coaching gymnastics, I would take note of an individual's upper and lower body strength, flexibility, endurance, power, proprioception etc., but it would be unhelpful to spend time making specific diagnostic categories for the athlete. (Ex: UncoordinatedStrongArm Disorder criteria = high pullup ability with average flexibility, above average power and below average coordination with a calm conditioning style.) I would then have to spend time debating whether slightly vs. very below average coordination warrants a different diagnosis ... instead of making note of the deficiencies, training the athlete, and modifying the plans as the athlete improved in their own individual manner. Their "disorder" would be a waste of time to pinpoint, but certainly their response to my training program would be noteworthy! I am interested in what the athlete can do, not what "disorder" I can make them fit into.

Even if a precise biomarker were discovered for each discrete mental illness, the therapeutic weapons for each person would dramatically vary in the same way that a vehicular traction control failure on an F-150 patrolling a beach would decree its driver in a vastly different predicament than that of the traction control failure of an Audi on an icy traffic circle in Minnesota.

Chapter 14

$$\begin{vmatrix} 1 & 0 & 0 \\ 0 & 1 & 0 \\ 0 & 0 & 1 \end{vmatrix}$$

RELENTLESS TORMENT

Beckoning me to follow, the shadowy suicidal summoning dagger stabbed me once again, and I had to battle those vile, vitriolic accusations of the futility and incomprehensible burden of life. I had resolved to perpetually and fervently decline to believe a word, but could barely stand beneath the onslaught. The pattern reemerged of confusion about how this existence works and how my entity could exist within this strange looking body, comprised of trillions of cells but with one distinct purpose and soul.

How exactly is it that I am typing this sentence right now, when I feel like my mind is in a vice and my soul is somewhere hidden behind my body? Why doesn't anyone else seem to understand?

Even Joe, having chosen to leave this planet, had retained his remarkable ability to comfort me with his voice. If he had shot me, I surely would have been traumatized, but the psychological bond I had formed with him was and is truly indestructible. It lies in a different dimension than our own. I became obsessed with analyzing his behavior for signs of an impending suicide.

I am imagining that you as the reader may find it strange that I have obsessed over these following messages so greatly. But visualize how someone who literally was taking away your pain suddenly not only died, but decided to die, the person who would ask you solemnly whether you felt suicidal would lose his own battle to that villain. I have two voice messages, one text message, and some emails from him. I listen to those voice messages over and over. The first comes from his returning my initial therapy inquiry call and goes exactly like this (perhaps the world's most boring message, but how I would yearn for boredom over despair):

Joe: "Hey this message is for Allison. This is Joe giving you a call, um from I believe Monday. When you get a chance, give me a call back at _______________ That's ___________ (number is repeated). Thanks."

Nothing too special to note here, but he was hopeful, a young practitioner having recently opened a practice and likely enthusiastic for clients to find him ...

The second message that I have was from him cancelling my appointment on one Friday in February. This is the exact transcript, which reads February 8, 2019 at 9:11 AM, length 27 seconds.

Joe: "Hey Allison. It's Joe giving you a call today on Friday morning. Uhh I'm actually in my car on my way back home, uhh, because (slight pause) I became suddenly quite ill this morning while in the office, and um it does <u>not</u> look like I'll *be able to uh stay at all. So I am very sorry about that, uh (brief sighing sound) Give me a call back when you get this, um, just so that we can confirm our next appointment. That's ___________ (phone number). Thanks."*

Predictably, this one I listen to more regularly than the first. This wasn't the day that he left the planet, but I couldn't help but wonder what his emotional state was like when he cancelled this appointment. How sick was he that day? What kind of sickness strikes so suddenly such that you have to leave work? The flu can sort of do that I suppose. He didn't sound ill, though. GI distress? Maybe, but usually that is sort of transient, and you can't predict that you would have to cancel your entire day. Pain? Perhaps. Whatever it was, I feel so bad for him and that I only took from him without giving back (besides money, which seems completely incomparable).

My new psychologist, David, has truly been a life saver. Joe was indubitably correct about him. At the conclusion of that last therapy appointment before Joe's death, as Joe began to shut his office door behind me, I had abruptly remembered how I had wanted to thank him for referring my husband and me to David. Pivoting, I peered back through the narrowing gap and announced how grateful we were for this referral. "He seems awesome," I noted. Joe's eyes briefly met mine with a solemn solidarity, then he fleetingly diverted his gaze and in a muffled tone uttered his deferential feelings about David. Joe had unquestionably known that I feared that if my psychologist couldn't conceptualize my tormenting obsessions, that I would deem myself not diseased at all, but instead believe to have discovered the clandestine horror movie that is this reality. In accord with Joe's assertion, what David spouts during sessions is scrupulous and insightful, and it is healingly challenging to try to outwit him. I had previously thought that the shouts in my head could insidiously outsmart anyone. Just hearing David's perceptive comments invokes peace, as if in response to the most euphonious concoction of string instruments serenading the entrapment of the vile cranial Apples to Apples beasts, who dissolve into a tranquil shoreline amidst the backdrop of an amethyst and ginger twilight.

Chapter 15

$$\begin{vmatrix} 1 & 0 & 0 \\ 0 & 1 & 0 \\ 0 & 0 & 1 \end{vmatrix}$$

THE DOG

Challenge: Which dog appears to be the one with the mental illness?

Beyond the city limits was a small animal shelter, in which four mournful puppies huddled together in a weathered cage. The howls of the distressed adult dogs and the lonesomeness of the cats simmered with the putrid stench of soiled concrete and the yelping of the forlorn pups.

In having read anecdotal accounts of dog ownership providing innumerable health benefits to owners, with some even expressing that their canine has kept them alive amidst suicidal ideation, it seemed fitting to invest in such a miraculous creature for my husband. I had found a sweet puppy's face online at a local animal shelter who had been dumped with his three siblings. We had wanted to adopt a puppy instead of an adult dog, because our family includes goats and ducks and figured it would be easier to train a young dog to respect (not eat) them. On this we were not wrong. I also thought it would be relatively easy to teach a dog to mind. On this I was far from correct.

The first clue that something was awry was at approximately 8 weeks of age. Our pup, Josiah, would start growling menacingly, hair standing on end, if we came within four feet of his dear food bowl. Resource guarder—no problem ... quite common in dogs. We could deal with that. We worked tirelessly to train him that we presented no threat to him. Perhaps his siblings had been jerks around the food bowl and he was traumatized by his lack of a fair share of food. So I would approach gingerly while he ate; he would stiffen and scarf faster, holding his tail close to his little body, while I tossed little bits of chicken into his bowl. Like clockwork, he began to appreciate my presence when eating, even allowing me to pet him. But as he grew, he began to develop other irrational fears, and he never really acclimated to my husband's unwelcome presence around the food bowl. We started hand feeding him, but the pup would get angry when my husband's hand was depleted of food, and bite his hand out of frustration over the oh-so-quickly depleting food supply. The following list includes what else causes the pup to erupt in rage:

1. Attempting to repossess anything, especially socks ... (He has been known to bite my husband over a precious pair of socks that is just too peerless to surrender.)

2. Cleaning. Cleaning anything at all. Pup loathes all forms of cleaning, and will bite your hand, if he can reach it, while you wipe off countertops. You certainly cannot clean the floor with him around. He pops a fuse and runs barking, ferociously biting your hand if you're wiping the ground.

3. Staring. Don't stare at any inanimate objects. Ever. It makes him totally freak out. If you are staring at a spot on the ground, wall, etc., he gazes inquisitively at you for a moment, and then starts growling and lunges to bite a hand.

4. Working on anything that touches the ground- for instance, my husband was working on our washing machine, and because he was fixated on the appliance, pup decided it would be another good thing to guard. This must be the most lackluster thing for a pup to have ever guarded.

5. Cleaning up his waste. He was relatively easy to train, but for any accidents, he will guard his excrement and bull rush anyone brave enough

to approach the zone. One night, he fashioned such a zone in the living room while we slept, and we awakened the next morning to him guarding his malodorous mound. (It lay directly outside of the bedroom door, which was open.) That recalcitrant canine wouldn't let my husband nor myself out of the bed. He would run around the bed barking menacingly and growling. We eventually won. My husband was able to grab the floor lamp beside the bed, snag the vacuum cleaner, and drag it over to the bed, then use the vacuum cleaner (which he does fear), to chase him out of the area.

6. At the top of the list is sheet moving. Pup cannot be allowed on the bed, because if he feels the sheet shift (like if you pull up the sheet because it got bunched), he growls and lunges with amazing cougar prowess to latch onto my husband's hand with frightening determination and tenacity. Don't ever move a blanket or sheet beneath him. Needless to say, we became terrified of him and began walking around the house with our hands literally above our heads,

as he seems to generally only have a hand-biting affinity.

Another day, sneaking past us on the way out of the door, he scampered into the street, only to be almost bulldozed by a passing car. He initially looked frightened and perplexed, tail curled beneath him, and then stopped and shot the car a look of disbelief and ultimately, vitriol. He then lunged at the car, which had stopped to ensure he was alright, and when the car began moving, he barked threateningly and chased it away. It kept going, so assuredly he had won. With a satisfied grunt, he plodded back to the porch.

He seems to have always had an edge, but the intensity did increase significantly when the vet prescribed Prozac for him. His guarding behavior escalated, and his face was more indefatigably frozen in a masked emotionless frame of fury. This somewhat abated after discontinuing the medication. He also has been better about the biting with age and after having been neutered, but he was still guarding and albeit not biting as readily, barking like a crazed beast and shoving my husband with his paws. So another vet prescribed Xanax and Trazodone for him. He began taking Xanax, and we finally could relax, as his temperament went from Sasquatch to irritable badger.

Regarding the mental issues, it is first fascinating to imagine the types of mental illness that can exist within other mammals. Further, you will recall that I had originally been prescribed Xanax, and how it had an addictive property after only a couple of weeks. Apparently, it's not that hard of a medication to acquire. The vet has prescribed the Xanax, 1mg tablets to take twice per day, with 6 refills! Although I would never even dream of taking a medication prescribed to my dog, it's somewhat unnerving for the taunting benzos to be just sitting there in the cabinet. Perhaps veterinarians should do mental health checks on owners when prescribing psychotropic drugs for their pup patients.

Besides being a traumatic experience, how does the sordid puppy relate to the benefit of therapy? Interestingly, we adopted a second dog, who has had a powerfully positive effect on Josiah's aggressive behavior. Similar to humans in therapy, *finding someone who can communicate with you on a deep level allows for lasting understanding and growth.* In this case, the communication came in the form of another creature with sharp teeth.

Answer to Challenge Question: The Hound

Chapter 16

$$\begin{vmatrix} 1 & 0 & 0 \\ 0 & 1 & 0 \\ 0 & 0 & 1 \end{vmatrix}$$

COVID.

I write this for my own future benefit. I am so grateful to be alive, to feel the steady warmth of the sun smile down upon my shoulders, to breathe deeply the crisp air and to know that I am healthy—that I have a purpose to impact the lives of my students each day. I am so thankful to have been given life and to have survived everything. There is a deep well of joy in my stomach and an unfathomable calmness in my mind that I have never known. I will keep looking back at this should I ever doubt that I have felt this way.

This gleeful feeling melted again into a pit of disconsolate torment. The thoughts took different forms, as I attempted to hold my head above water and repel the darts. Screaming in my mind was that voice that claimed that it would be better to cease treading water and drown. Every second was taxing, it said, and at moments I would believe it. It took away every glimmer of hope I had and stated that no optimism would ever return. I despaired to the point of desert enervation. The sky had turned to ink, and my soul felt void. Fathoming another second of the onslaught heightened the panic. But the thunderclaps began to reduce in decibels and the lightning became less frequent, and once again, I rejoiced in having survived. It is a fight worth every drop of sweat and blood for the triumph of the cup of peace. With therapy, the suicidal feelings would waltz with the feeling of elation, each dancer alternating traipses into the light for a spell of time.

$

The world then transformed. It was 7:03pm. As I finished a late-night dinner pedagogy meeting on campus, a colleague came into the room and declared, "I'm guessing you all haven't seen the email yet ... "

And there it was. Spring break had just ended, and I had taught Anatomy that day. But classes were cancelled for the remainder of the week, and all in-person classes were to be cancelled for the rest of

March, and possibly for the entire semester (and as you well know, they indeed were). So I began online teaching—participated in a dizzying number of Zoom calls, and ardently tried to connect with my students in a meaningful way despite the circumstances. Initially, watching others begin to wash hands repeatedly and check themselves constantly for symptoms of the disease was somewhat validating. I had spent my entire life doing such things, and now the entire world was doing it, too.

Perhaps now everyone would understand.

For whatever reason, a month later, my brain felt like it capsized. The one-year anniversary of Joe's death was impending, and I began to obsess over reasons that he may have taken his life. The internal voices screamed at me that it was too strenuous to exist ... to take each breath ... to move even slightly. How much ATP is needed for me to even just sit here? Am I peaceful enough with just silent consciousness to want to do this indefinitely?

If I were an astronaut lost in space and inexplicably had a suit that would keep me alive eternally without food or water, but I would never meet another human, and there was a red button I could press to die at any time, do I love the feeling of consciousness enough to never in eternity press the red button?

How can I know!? I MUST KNOW! I geared up to go to war with the taunts in my head, but in doing so slid farther down into a pit of despair and painful perplexity.

How was I alive? Why had so many people in my life killed themselves recently? Should it be hard to be alive? At every moment, I would keep asking myself, "Why do I want to be alive? Am I sure that I want to be alive?" And "Is it too hard to be alive? Think of all of the energy expenditure it takes to just utter a simple phrase? How have I been able to do that my entire life!? It seems so confusing and exhausting." A strangling sensation laughed and pranced around my neck and my mind, such that it felt like all power in my being was being used to just maintain consciousness. Could I upright my ship and handle this indefinitely?

During this period, I became so jittery and troubled that I stopped sleeping more than 1 or 2 hours per night and spent every day either running, doing some other intense exercise, or going on drives around and around the city for hours. Friends expressed to me that they barely saw any change to their odometers during the stay-at-home order. But I drove thousands of miles, because I couldn't bear to sit still. At times I would sprawl on the floor and scream in panic, and the rest of the time grit my teeth, try to ignore the shouting in my head and the choking sensation around my neck, and sprint or drive.

"Do you need to go to the hospital?" Jay posited.

I truly wasn't sure. The local psychiatric hospital has a place where you can be evaluated and ask questions if you just walk in. So I went. I wanted to know if I was in danger. I felt like every second was too dreadful, so I worried about my life. Upon arrival, there was a basic vitals room where the initial interrogation occurred, after which I was escorted through hefty, tarnished doors into a main triage area that looked like a small version of an Emergency Room. They informed me that due to the pandemic, my husband would not be permitted back there. That was alarming, but I followed through those perilous doors. A central desk separated the calm staff from the perturbed patients perched on the shabby chairs aligning the battered walls ... I signed some forms ... I began to sense the reality of the entrapment ... I didn't want to be there anymore. I tore from my chair and approached a nurse:

"You know what? I feel better. I don't think I need to be here."

Nurse: "I'm sorry. You signed the forms, so you have to stay until you speak to the doctor."

I couldn't remain there. Shock enshrouded, and I had to get out. Could I ask to get something from my car and then drive away? Surely they had heard that one before. My clever (so I believed) brain was betraying me for good escape strategies. Could I break through those glass doors? Probably not quickly enough to not be sedated in my maniacal efforts.

Gliding out from behind the doors was a towering doctor, my potential source of freedom. The first thing I noticed when he came to get me was that he made immediate, purposeful eye contact, locking eyes with me for an uncomfortably prolonged period of time. I had 0.3 seconds to determine what a sane gaze might look like ... I chose one and tried to peer in his eyes with concern but steadiness. The other patients' eyes had appeared to dart spasmodically. In the room, he tranquilly asked why I found myself there, and I explained the fear of harming myself. He began to reassure me that often OCD and anxiety manifest in this way. Suddenly screams arose over the loudspeaker and he gusted, "Medical Emergency—be right back!" He sprinted out of the room.

I sat fearful and impatient for his return. He burst back into the room and beseeched me about my "ego dystonic" (feelings that don't feel like me) notions. He let me go, thankfully, ruling once again that I was a delusional but safe patient. I am grateful that this place exists; everyone working there was fabulously kind and conscientious, but I was positively delighted to not find myself there.

This season of torment possessed a slight disparity from those of the past. A splinter of hope that had not been present before had slashed through. Going to therapy was powerful enough to provide brief but palpable solace. Little by little, the puzzle pieces in my mind began to interlock again, and the caustic thoughts slid off more slickly. The truth is that the illusion does indeed seem to be overthinking (a woeful form of overthinking that skillfully masquerades as involuntary), along with the deception of being forced to solve that problem in order to be safe. Certainly life is indeed bizarre. Consciousness is strikingly fascinating and requires much more energetic cost than seems feasible for an organism, and the energy expenditure we make daily even doing nothing is dizzying, but a lot of the time we autopilot and do those things without thinking.

Interestingly, the philosophical topics that have tried to destroy me, I can discuss just fine, *as long as they don't come from that sinister OCD place, and their entrance comes with a feeling that I have finally learned to recognize in therapy.*

I would summarize the recent thought assailants as follows:

Hostile thought 1: "You can't make it another second, and even if you could, you don't want to. What makes you think you're stronger than the others you knew who succumbed?"

Hostile thought 2: "Normal people enjoy living day to day, but this is horrifyingly arduous for you, as I have shown you that life is like running circles on a track, with each morning beginning the same drudgery as the last; each night transitions back to starting point A with no progress."

This cyclical nature of life feels tormenting. But it is an illusion. Of course, time is not really just a line either. For time dilation to be a potential physical possibility, there must be a way to "distort" time itself.

In fact, all of this was an illusion—a powerful one, yet an illusion nonetheless. I don't have any ability to keep myself thinking and functioning, and "I" am separate from the actions of my body's cells. My brain tends to send a confused and distressed message to itself if I look too far inward like this. Does yours? It is not hard to be alive if you're not obligated to legally prove why you don't think it is difficult. But if you are forced to perpetually craft such a defense, even blinking is excruciating in light of this trick.

And in the presence of therapy, something breaks apart about my urgency of solving life's puzzles. The interest endures, but the world feels more like a game, and one that I am fit to win.

$$\oint$$

Analyzing my dream world has also molded another tool for my armory. I have had many dreams that have seemed to manifest into reality, some of which I have told others in advance to verify that I don't mistakenly resurrect a false memory after something occurs. Do such experiences go along with being crazy, or am I noticing something abstruse? Sometimes it is something pointless and simple, ex: a snapshot of using my husband's old phone instead of my own the day before my phone ceased to function for no overt reason. Other examples include photo-like images of my dog breaking his foot days before this actually happened. One May, I dreamt that my husband was fired the second week of August and that the week prior, he had to call out of work. Three months later, my husband threw his back out and couldn't work, after which his email account was inaccessible. He tried to contact his boss to inquire, and I broke the news to him that he was likely getting fired ... He was indeed. He didn't do anything to be fired; they were just precipitously going in a different direction. These specific dreams are intriguingly devoid of color, with no perceptible emotion on my part, a positively wonderful feeling of simple observation without distress. Differentiating dream types has aided in my delineation of pathological thought types.

Regarding regular dreams that contain my tormenting thoughts, those lively ones evoked after a large pizza before bed, I have noticed an interesting pattern. Like the temperature delay of a lake, cooling gradually as the first freeze strikes and warming slowly after summer has pierced through, the nightly reveries do not match the state of my conscious mind. The October lake is still warm, and the May lake ice cold. When a suicidal state would strike, dreams became a welcome escape. Dream Alli would have "normal" thoughts and desires. As the mental agony would begin to lift, the dreams would metamorphose into hellish infernos boasting the shouting accusations that had recently been present during the conscious part of the day. What is the reason for this phenomenon!? Dreams that do not relate to my recent obsessions appear to be exempt from this liquid temperature change manifestation. If I watch a movie about tornadoes, I often dream about them that very evening. But if obsessed about the perilous dagger of time, for instance, I lament for weeks before the blades penetrate into my dreams.

Chapter 17

$$\begin{vmatrix} 1 & 0 & 0 \\ 0 & 1 & 0 \\ 0 & 0 & 1 \end{vmatrix}$$

THE DOOR

So what is it about therapy that has been so remarkably helpful? What is David's strategy? I am most appreciative of his desire to be very "in-the-moment" like a super sleuth searching for clues and capitalizing on them with insightful elucidations of possible underlying reasons behind each tormenting notion. In my extremely limited understanding of therapy practices, I appreciate that he isn't ever trying some newfangled smoke and mirrors strategy to have the pretense of doing something magical. For me, the magic is in his unyielding compassion and giftedness for understanding and challenging even the most convoluted thought processes, and his courage is captivating and contagious!

His strategy is like an adept gardener of the mind. Instead of just scouring for weeds to pull that may grow back with abandon, he treats the whole orchard, resolving to remove weeds gently while patiently treating the soil and promoting growth of the virtuous plants.

This will take time. I predict the annihilation of the castle of consternation and rebuilding of a fortress of peace and power will be an extensive but unfathomably worthwhile process.

I will now tell another story that illustrates how therapy has helped. It's actually a distressingly humiliating tale but shows my point well, I believe:

I was 12 and a half years old and in seventh grade. At my school in central Florida, seventh graders got to go on a grand field trip to the Florida Keys called Sea Camp. You get to take a city bus there, lather yourself in mud and play tag in the mangroves, snorkel, go on exotic boat rides, learn more about sea life ... a lot of things that you can do in central Florida as well, with the exception of the mangrove play. But as a field trip, this rocked. Also, there was something that I had never experienced before: shark swimming! They had sectioned off an area along the coast dedicated to hosting hammerhead sharks. As you may expect, many students were enthusiastic but fearful of bathing with the ferocious water beasts. It was a typically warm, sunny south Florida day, and all of the students perched on some rocks alongside this hammerhead habitation, half eager to dive in and half fearful/excited to re-emerge and claim that they swam with sharks. The voice of the young camp counselor leading our group rang out what was supposed to be a comforting announcement:

"There really is no danger in swimming with these hammerhead sharks. They don't really ever bite anyone. In fact, the only thing that would be unwise to do is to cut your finger and then splash your hand around in the water, as they could be attracted to the blood and bite your hand thinking that it is a struggling morsel of food."

But there was only one problem. I had just gotten my first period and was too embarrassed to tell anyone. I was bleeding pretty substantially and was expected to roam, possibly even swim, with those sharks ... and I didn't have anything to stop the bleeding. So I waded slowly inward, and while my friends splashed around cheerfully, I hovered near the bank, readying myself to fend off any attacking shark. I was poised for action at the slightest hint of a stealthily approaching hammerhead.

So in the current situation in which I found myself, there was really no choice but to wade into the shark infested waters.

What other opportunity did I have? Tell the counselor what was happening? Have everyone mock me? I think not! Maybe the seventh-grade student body would have been civilized. Not likely. As an adult revisiting the situation, I can obviously see other options. In keeping with the notion as I saw it at the time that I was in immediate danger, I didn't actually have to jump into the water with the sharks. There was a way out. There was another option. But the only one apparent at the time was to drape myself in armor and prepare myself for battle, to ward off sharks. This is what I have done for my entire life. I wake up in the morning and dress with my knight costume and jump into my worst-case scenario scenes and then battle tirelessly until dusk. I am certainly a proponent of fighting one's battle, but I had been engaging in the battles alone, rendering this a hopeless tournament.

Thus I have been trapped in these mental rooms with terrifying thrashing, assailing beasts, and they are always blocking the door that leads out. There was no other way out than to conceptualize and battle the thoughts. I have surveyed the rooms in which I have found myself for other ways out, for attics or evidence of secret passageways or even a skylight to which I could somehow ascend and break through. But there has never been an alternative to the combat.

... Until David built another door. I declare that there has never been another door before, no hope of escape, but now another door has begun to take form beside the one blocked by the behemoths. I fight for the ability to conceptualize the peaceful feeling that accompanies being in his office and install it atop the perpetual gnawing fear. I am being greeted with the choice to dive back into the world of disarray or to bask in that tranquility and empowerment and fight from a different vantage point. The choice is still not easy somehow, which is somewhat backward. I do have to fight with all of my strength to ignore the yanking of the creatures to pull me back into the room, to not fall for the deception of their ghastly beckoning. But with each day, the balancing atop of the platform of peace becomes more natural, and the door leading out of the beast chamber increases in pigment. Sometimes I still feel like my consciousness has been collapsed into a single point below my ears and that my body is this floating concoction of confounding chaos, but then reappears that ever-sharpening outline of that door that had been previously simply theoretical. I am eternally grateful.

§

Free Will and OCD

I have found it to be difficult to end a book. I could quote a poignant verse or attempt to dazzle you with a well-constructed and poetic summarizing statement to end this tale. Instead I will break my rule about this book having no literature citations and make a comment about something I have noticed about OCD after having read about some of the recent research articles whose results could potentially challenge our notion of free will. The first paper I read about the concept essentially had participants select and imagine one of two different images (something like horizontal or vertical stripes)[2]. These participants were encouraged to choose one of those two images to visually imagine. Participants were permitted to take their time to choose their desired image. (They generally made their selection within 5 seconds.) Afterward, participants were instructed to imagine whichever image they chose, as intensely as possible, for 10 seconds. Next, buttons would appear on the screen prompting the participants to select which image they had been thinking about. During this whole "choosing a picture and imagining it" process, participants' "brain activity" was being recorded with functional magnetic resonance imaging (fMRI), which basically makes use of the fact that oxygen consumption changes in the brain in regions where there is increased energetic need (presumably resulting from neuronal firing variations). This change in oxygen consumption, as well as the increased blood flow to the area (to provide oxygen), causes a change in magnetic field that can be easily imaged[3]. Researchers in this study analyzed these fMRI data from participants choosing and imagining their selected images to try to determine whether there were any patterns that would help them detect which image the participants chose (without asking them). They used a machine learning algorithm, which sounds fancy, but just means that they analyzed the data to try to predict, via a sort of logical decision tree, which brain patterns most likely go with which type of image. They claim statistically significant ability to do this, but most interestingly, it appeared as though the "thought patterns" that went along with each of the images were developing as long as 11 seconds prior to the participants attesting that they had chosen! Moreover, it looked as though the "vertical stripe pattern brain activity" was active 11 seconds before the person professed "I have chosen the vertical stripe pattern!"

My initial thought about this work, and those that were similar, was that this type of "choice" (choosing random images), was the type of decision-making activity in which the subconscious workings of the mind may very well take over. Given the lack of any existential value to these types of decisions, perhaps the brain creates its own "random number generator" or "random image generator" that appears somewhat unpredictable and is outside of the consciousness. This type of behavior may be useful if you are running through the woods, escaping that aforementioned assailing bear. Your brain's choosing which trees to dodge around may be less predictable to the bear, and more energetically favorable to you, if your conscious self is not directly steering the ship. But then again, perhaps at some point in your life, you semi-consciously created such a generator that may work well in these types of situations, in the same way a person writes a computer code. You consciously write the computer code, but once it's written, it executes quickly without your guiding hand and just gives you the result. (But you were at one time responsible for programming the internal decision tree guidelines.)

What has truly vexed me, however, was not necessarily the spooky concept that our conscious mind may not always be doing the choosing, but because this strikes a chord close to what it feels like to "have OCD." It has truly felt to me as though when a tormenting OCD-type thought manifests, that there was a fabrication of this thought some time before I detected it, probably roughly 10 seconds prior. There is a feeling of internal contemplation mixed with intense panic as I wait for whatever the thought stemming from this deranged brain computer program will vitriolically reveal. And then that grievous thought hits, and I consciously must gear up to slay it. If the thought, for example, is like "Go bash your head against that wall as hard as you can," it truly feels as though this is the chosen behavior of my body, but not me. My brain has chosen; and as soon as I become aware of this choice, I am appalled and must fight it. But with what? Thence arise the compulsions. The compulsions soothe for this reason: they are part of the battle to commandeer the brain's aberrant computer codes. It's like banging systematically on the vending machine to dislodge the stuck soda. It works.

Stopping the compulsions without changing the codes is pointless and precarious. It is with the clever rewriting of these previously nefarious codes that David has begun to transform my reality, empowering me to begin to thrive. I will continue to heal.

Fight Strategically.

References

[1]Framingham, J. (2018). Minnesota Multiphasic Personality Inventory (MMPI). Psych Central. Retrieved on August 19, 2020, from https://psychcentral.com/lib/minnesota-multiphasic-personality-inventory-mmpi/

[2]Koenig-Robert, R., & Pearson, J. (2016). Decoding the nonconscious dynamics of thought generation. doi:10.1101/090712

[3]Glover, G. H. (2011). Overview of Functional Magnetic Resonance Imaging. Neurosurgery Clinics of North America, 22(2), 133-139. doi:10.1016/j.nec.2010.11.001

Acknowledgements

I am wholly thankful for the unending support and prayers of my family and dear friends, who have helped me keep fighting. My marvelous mom was the first to see me tattered by fear, and she was always there to comfort and elevate. My brilliant dad has always made me feel like there was nothing ever that I could not conquer. My amazing stepmom was the first to get psychological help for me, which has been a massive turning point in my life. My delightful husband is my best friend, and I can't fathom a more perfect soul. I am forever grateful for his instrumental role in bringing forth the best in this book. Further, I am appreciative of the benevolent and professional writing advice from our cherished family friend, Professor Fred Ashe. I am grateful for the innovative support of Dr. Becker, Dr. McGuire, and Dr. Sprick, and for their assiduousness in unearthing novel data. I am of course thankful to Joe for being the first to clinically engage in warfare with me for my mind. He was/is a very compassionate and insightful professional. Indelibly, I am incomprehensibly thankful to Dr. David Sacks for his valiant wisdom, unrivaled discernment, and indefatigability.

כבד אלהים הסתר דבר וכבד מלכים חקר דבר

The following pages present part of my animal support team, who object far less to being photographed than the more helpful humans.

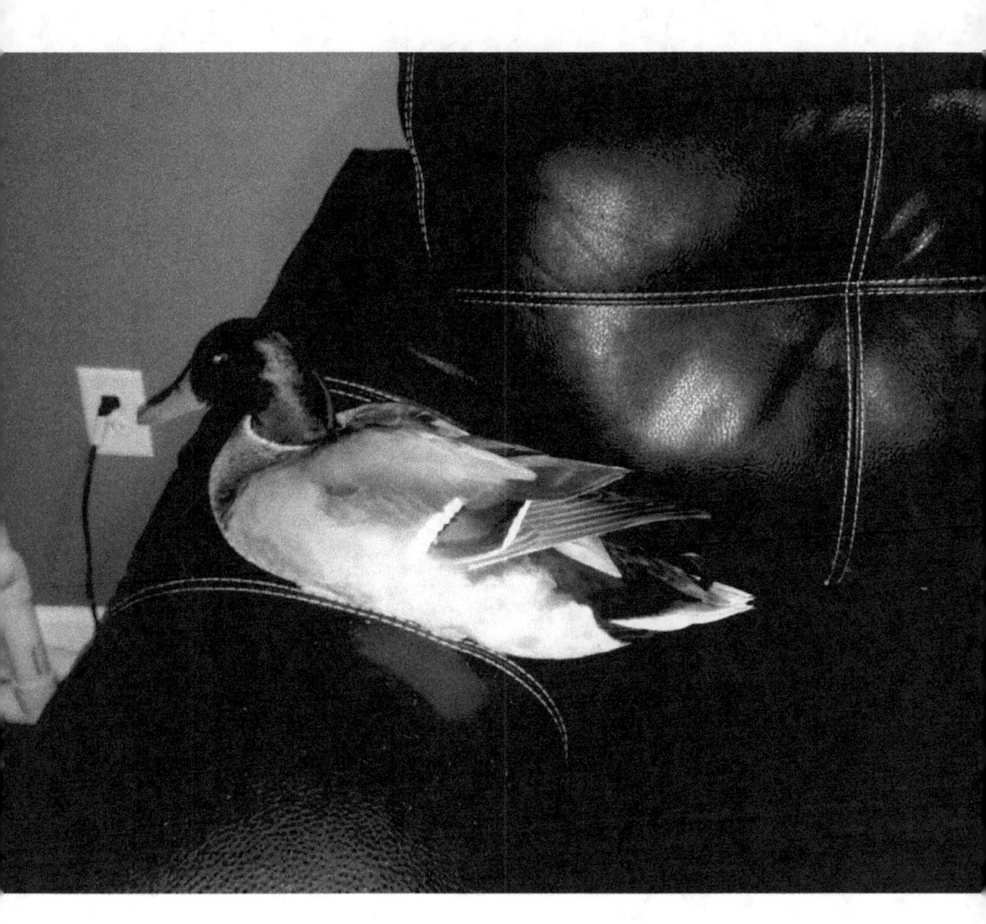